Process Politics:
A Guide for Group Leaders

Process Politics:
A Guide for Group Leaders

Eileen Guthrie
Warren Sam Miller

University Associates, Inc.
8517 Production Avenue
P.O. Box 26240
San Diego, CA 92126

Copyright © 1981 by International Authors, B.V.
ISBN: 0-88390-167-6
Library of Congress Catalog Card Number 81-51484
Printed in the United States of America

PREFACE

This book, formerly entitled *Making Change,* is for people who are members of groups. More precisely, it is for people who want to bring about positive change through democratic processes.

The purpose of this book is to provide a conceptual framework as well as concrete tools for *process politicians*—change agents whose expertise is in the area of group dynamics and decision making.

The principles of process politics were developed as a result of our experiences with task-oriented groups in a variety of settings, including inner-city neighborhoods, southern Appalachia, Indian reservations, rural midwestern communities, social-service agencies, volunteer organizations, businesses, universities, and religious organizations. These principles are equally applicable in any setting in which groups or group members interact, whether in the public sector, the private sector, or the so-called "third sector" of nonprofit organizations.

In this book we have used a leadership-development approach that is oriented toward teaching people the skills they need to gain power and to manage change in their lives. We intentionally have not focused on specific change issues; instead, we have chosen to focus on skills and concepts that can be adapted to *any* issue and *any* group situation.

The two of us represent different viewpoints regarding the application of process politics. Eileen sees process politics as a tool for advocating and supporting the development of grass-roots leadership; she believes that with appropriate assistance, people who see themselves as victims of institutional and bureaucratic systems can develop the self-confidence essential for bringing about long-range social change.

In contrast, Sam is interested in empowerment at all levels rather than just at the grass-roots level. His experience has shown that all people benefit from a sense of increasing the control they have over their own lives. The framework he uses to look at the process of empowerment is called *human-energy management*—or the ways in which people make use of their energy as individuals, in relationships with others, and in groups.

Each of us wants to specially mention the people who have taught us the most about what we call process politics. Thanks from Eileen are extended to Barbara Anderson-Sannes, Bill Grimberg, Kebie Hatcher, the late Glenna Krause, Margaret Macneale, Orville Mestes, Sam Miller, Mike Roan, and Dennis Wynne. Sam wishes to thank Betty Aldridge, Hartz Brown, Mike Groh, the late Bristow Hardin, Don Klein, daughters Brenda and Laurie, parents Levi and Nina Miller, Carl Smith, David Rogers, and Wheelock Whitney.

We hope that the ideas offered in this book are helpful to all people who work to make groups more effective. Also, as more and more people begin to understand the importance of the ways in which decisions are made, we hope that together we can all contribute to creating and implementing our visions for our lives, both individually and collectively.

We welcome thoughts, comments, and criticisms about the material included in this book.

Eileen Guthrie and Sam Miller
Minneapolis, Minnesota
August, 1981

CONTENTS

CHAPTER 1

INTRODUCTION TO PROCESS POLITICS: A WAY TO THINK ABOUT CHANGE

Process politics is an approach that groups, organizations, and communities can use to get things done in a way that incorporates accomplishment and personal fulfillment. It recognizes that individuals and groups share a desire to be *political*—to influence events that affect them and to manage change in ways that lead to success and prosperity. The *process* aspect of process politics involves a perspective that the methods used to get things done are as important as the goals; the end does not justify the means. Achieving goals, even lofty goals, means little if people feel belittled, embarrassed, or frustrated by the way in which things are done.

Process politics helps people influence change through effective group action. It involves leadership roles and techniques that strengthen group effectiveness by using the self-interests of group members, expressed through broadly based decision making and concerted action. The human concerns of group members are not in conflict with task-oriented activities. Rather, these concerns can be combined with group activities in a manner that benefits everyone. When that happens, both individuals and groups are empowered in that they have a greater sense of being in control of events that affect them.

This book includes theory and techniques, learned from formal training and practical experience, about ways to bring about change through effective group action. It is based on several premises that facilitate effectiveness in working with people:

- Everybody counts.
- Feelings are facts.
- An individual's perceptions are true, for that person.
- Self-interest is okay.
- Power is amoral, neither good nor bad.

- Diversity is valuable in decision making.
- People can solve their own problems.

CHANGE: FRAMEWORK FOR ACTION

It is important that groups and group leaders understand change. Change is inherently neither positive nor negative, but it may be either when viewed from the perspective of a particular situation. As Toffler (1970) has stated, we live in a time of rapid and accelerating change, for individuals, relationships, organizations, and cultures.

The key issue in understanding change is not to decide whether change itself is good or bad but to examine the effect that a specific change will have on the needs, values, goals, and interests of a group. This task is sometimes difficult because the self-interests and goals of individual members may be in direct conflict with each other (see Chapter 9).

New approaches to managing change are needed at all levels of decision making. Often change has been directed toward the benefit of small groups of people with vested interests in the outcomes, and too many people have felt like losers with regard to the changes that affect their lives. The element that appears to have been lacking in the past is a perspective that could open up the management of change to large numbers of people and provide a group with access to the problem-solving energies of its own members.

Approaches to Change

Because change affects everyone, most people have a desire to manage it by influencing events in a way that brings reality together with their values and perceptions. Regardless of whether change is considered to be happening too slowly or too quickly, attempts to speed up or slow down its course are always involved in change management. The notion of organizing our thinking about change so that we can influence its course is not a new one; many people over the years have used different approaches to manage change in order to bring about desired results or to resist undesirable ones.

The perspective of process politics is to recognize that it is unlikely that any single strategy for managing change will be effective in all situations. It is useful to avoid the tendency to limit oneself to any single strategy and to concentrate instead on building a repertoire of approaches such as the following.

1. Many groups use a *democratic* format for managing change, in which all members participate in defining concerns and making decisions. This approach is effective in situations in which the issues are sufficiently uncomplicated and the group size is small enough to make full participation possible. It has the advantage of enhancing each member's sense of involvement and ownership of the group's activities and concerns, but it loses effectiveness with increasing group size or when the issues are complex. The New England town meeting, an example of this approach involving decisions that are open to all residents (or members), is used by many organizations.

2. When a group is too large or the issues too complex for every member to be involved, a *representative* format is often more productive. With this approach some of the analysis, planning, and decision making is done by a smaller group of people who have been chosen to speak for the larger group. These people may represent the total group membership, as in the case of a board of directors that is chosen from the membership at large, or they may speak for a selected portion of the membership, as in the case of those selected to represent a geographical area or a special-interest group. The representative approach to managing change enables decisions to be made in larger, more complex situations; it requires the sensitivity of representative decision makers to their constituents and can break down if the representatives become insensitive or isolated.

3. The *appeal to authority* is another approach to managing change. When difficulties emerge in a group or negative outside influences result in an impasse, groups sometimes find it necessary to turn to someone recognized by all factions as an authority in the matters at hand. The authority can either be internal (as in the case of a manager in the organization involved) or external (as when a problem is taken to the courts for resolution). This approach is especially useful in situations in which conflict has reached an intensity that will not allow for rational discussion of the issues or when adversaries are not able to find enough common ground to provide a basis for discussion. Arbitration of labor/management disputes is an example of managing change by appealing to authority.

4. Another approach to managing change is *passive resistance.* This approach uses noncooperation as the strategy for calling attention to perceived injustices and thereby forcing action. Labor-union strikes illustrate this strategy, as does the civil-disobedience tactic

advocated by the late Dr. Martin Luther King, Jr., in which racial injustice was challenged through use of the boycott and nonviolent action.

5. *Confrontation* is also a viable approach to managing change. When a person or group feels totally powerless or oppressed, direct confrontation is sometimes considered to be the only course of action. Alinsky (1971) developed a framework for planning social action using the confrontation model, in which people who felt excluded, powerless, and oppressed forced change by disrupting business as usual until the status quo was changed.

6. *Self-help* strategies can be used to manage change in cases in which people must take an active role in improving their own situations. For example, an employer who wants to gain control of spiraling health-care costs might involve employees in planning ways to encourage healthy life styles. Opportunities might be developed for people to learn ways to feel better, and resources might be provided to support life-style changes.

7. The women's movement and evangelical Christianity are two examples of a *consciousness-raising* approach to achieving change. This model assumes that broad change occurs only after individual values have been changed. Under this philosophy organized efforts at social and political change are considered less important than personal enlightenment.

Valuable elements exist in all of these change-management approaches; but, in and of itself, each approach is inadequate. The perspective of process politics is that strategies for managing change differ with differing situations. With this perspective it is possible to avoid the tendency to limit oneself to any single strategy and to choose approaches that are appropriate.

The Importance of Groups in Managing Change

Groups and collections of groups are the backbone of most organizational decision-making structures. They may be formal and visible, such as a board of directors or a legislative body, or they may be less structured, such as an ad-hoc planning committee with no ultimate authority but with a recognized role in the policy-making process.

Not everyone has the interest, time, or optimism to work for change. Those who are so inclined generally increase their potential for success by joining with others who have similar concerns. This principle is true regardless of whether the situation is in the business, public, or community sector.

Members of groups can help change things that are going badly. They can take initiative to form still other groups to solve shared problems; they can enlist help from other groups and individuals; they can form coalitions to exert political pressure, set up study groups to delve into complex questions and recommend solutions, or call press conferences to publicize the need for changes in public policy.

Effectively working for change through groups calls for knowledge of how groups operate and how to apply these principles of operation to enhance group effectiveness. (An overview of basic group dynamics is included in Chapter 5.)

A group is a collection of people who choose to interact around their common needs. Completing the following inventory will help you categorize the groups to which you belong.

☐

Group-Affiliation Inventory

Take a few minutes to think about the groups to which you belong and list them according to the following categories:

1. Groups that other people know about:

2. Groups that other people do not know about:

3. Groups toward which you feel the greatest commitment:

4. Groups to which you devote the most time:

5. Groups that you would prefer not to belong to:

☐

As you read the following list of suppositions about groups, consider the groups that you listed. You might disagree with some of these suppositions, and you might be able to make additions.

1. *A group's members have more differences than similarities.* Each member of a group has had a unique set of experiences from which he or she has developed a personal knowledge base and certain feelings and beliefs. For example, Don and Elizabeth are both members of the same neighborhood organization and live in the same apartment building. But when the downstairs tenant, an American Indian, was evicted, Elizabeth was happy that the building no longer housed an Indian, whereas Don was angered and accused the landlord of discrimination.

2. *People in a group cannot always be expected to agree on what is "right" and what is "wrong."* Even though group members share some common needs, they do not have everything in common. For example, arguments may break out in families, and members of the Parent-Teacher Association may disagree on the degree to which

schools should be involved in sex education. Decisions depend on building agreement among a group's members.

3. *In every group some things are going well.* Often a group's members forget to consciously look for what is going well within the group so that they can preserve the positive features. For example, the board of directors of a company might be bogged down in disagreements over whether or not to expand into a new product line. It is important for the members of such a group to remember that, although they are having some difficulties in reaching agreement, their ability to level with each other and explore alternatives and conflicts is a positive factor that needs to be continued beyond that particular decision.

4. *In every group some things are going badly.* All of us must recognize that no group is perfect and, in fact, that all groups experience periods during which things do not go well.

5. *Each group exists in a larger context.* Events that happen outside a group can directly affect that group; conversely, events within a group can have an external effect. To put it simply, no group exists in a vacuum. Groups combine to form larger groups, which, in turn, interface with other systems through the interactions of their individual members or in their capacities as organizational entities.

6. *Groups are not effective in isolation.* As just mentioned, groups are part of larger organizations, systems, and networks. They exist in relationship to other groups and must be viewed in that context when decisions are made. Sometimes they have little control over those other groups; more often, however, the keys to change are dependent upon their interaction.

7. *Groups grow, learn, and develop.* They go through phases of development that in many ways parallel the stages of human development. A newly formed committee, for instance, is dependent on its leader (parent) for guidance and nurturing. As the group develops, a period of rebellion against the leader usually occurs (adolescence), followed by a period of cooperation (maturity). This developmental phenomenon is sometimes re-experienced as new members are brought in and old members leave or as issues change.

PROCESS POLITICS: THE ART OF THE POSSIBLE

As a body of techniques, process politics draws on the change-management approaches previously discussed, placing importance on the following goals:

1. *To influence institutional, as well as individual, causes of problems.* For example, consider a situation in which a city council has received five phone calls within the past two days complaining about the way in which food stamp recipients are treated at the local welfare office. One way of looking at the situation would be to demand that the present staff be fired; the process-politics approach would be to examine how much of the situation is caused by bad policy and needs to be addressed from that standpoint if the problem, and not just its symptoms, is to be resolved.

2. *To encourage self-determination.* In process politics, groups need to recognize and build on their own expertise and skills as much as possible. They need to decide for themselves what their futures will be. People grow and learn best when they have the opportunity to determine their own successes as well as failures.

3. *To increase cooperation within and among groups.* Although modern methods of travel and communication sometimes make the world seem small, we often do not know what is happening down the block, much less across town. Because the actions of one group could potentially affect another group, process politics encourages communications and regular contact between groups interested in the same problems. Without such opportunities for contact, groups might never discover whether their assumptions about each other's intents and purposes are accurate.

4. *To develop individual skills.* Frequently the aid of consultants and professionals is enlisted to help group members help themselves. However, many of these "experts" fail to teach group members the skills they need. Process politics emphasizes increasing group members' skills at problem solving and figuring out how to get what they want. In this way the potential for changes to be short lived and ineffective is diminished.

5. *To spread ownership of decisions by involving those affected in decision-making processes.* In process politics one characteristic of effective decisions is that they are permanent. In other words, those affected by a particular decision feel a strong commitment to it and work hard to follow through. Even "good" decisions are not carried out unless they have committed backers. With process politics it is considered essential that everyone's opinions are heard and built into group decisions.

6. *To value individual differences.* The decisions made by very diverse groups of people are often amazing in their richness. In process politics a high value is placed on having many different

kinds of people involved in deciding things; consequently, techniques are used that encourage such involvement.

THE FOUNDATION BLOCKS OF PROCESS POLITICS

Process politics is a set of assumptions and techniques intended to help groups manage their own processes of growth and to help group members become capable, effective problem solvers. The specific assumptions that serve as the foundation blocks of process politics are as follows:

1. *Problems are solvable.* Process politics can be thought of as "the art of the possible." Obviously, not all problems are immediately solvable; but the process politician maintains a basically optimistic attitude about people's abilities to figure out a logical way to approach difficult decisions.

2. *Both creative energy and pragmatism are essential components in problem solving.* It is important for groups to know what they want, what can be done now, and what can be done later. Creativity is important in helping to free people from tunnel-vision thinking, through which they unconsciously limit their options. Pragmatic thinking helps to keep groups in touch with realities that might make goal achievement either easier or more difficult.

3. *It is essential to pay attention to both long-term perspectives and short-term objectives.* Groups need to define their long-range goals, such as reducing employee turnover; but, unless they have short-term checkpoints along the way to gauge their progress, they may give up long before their final goals are accomplished. People need frequent payoffs if they are to continue working toward something.

4. *Any of a number of different approaches to change can be useful, depending on the situation and its dynamics.* Some people respond to consciousness-raising approaches, while others are more effectively involved through a self-help process. A group must decide which approach is most appropriate for a particular situation.

5. *People count.* They are more than numbers in any group. They have personalities and experiences that affect how they respond and what they contribute. This assumption means that it is important to notice people, to relate to them as individuals with individual wants, hopes, and fears. It is also important to relate to people as group members with group wants, hopes, and fears. For example, Bob James might very well be the director of the Marketing

Department, but he is also a human being who has good and bad days and who sometimes does not get home from meetings until 11 p.m.

6. *It is important to learn from what we do.* Sam tells a story about learning to ski. He decided that it was all right to fall down once because he looked the wrong way; but if he fell down twice because he looked the wrong way, that was stupid. Thus, groups should talk about what they are doing and why they make the choices they make. If something is going badly within a group, the members should analyze the situation and try to figure out a way to improve it. Also, if something has gone well within a group, it is important for its members to determine the reasons for their success.

A LOOK AT POWER

Power is a loaded word. Most people have emotionally charged responses when they are in situations with perceived power struggles. This principle is valid for one-to-one relationships as well as for groups.

We have been doing training for a number of years using the Power Lab (Oshry, 1975), a simulation of groups and community dynamics in which people belong to different groups in a workshop (see Chapter 11). These groups have unequal access to things that they need or want, such as food, space, beds, and so forth. One group has control over resources that the other groups want or need.

Many interesting things happen in the Power Lab. Very few people feel comfortable with the power differences, but one result is common to all groups: They respond. People experiment with various ways to achieve group cohesiveness and to influence other groups. Some become aggressive; others withdraw; others strategize. All of the models for managing change are tried. Sometimes groups use their power to help solve problems; often they have trouble knowing what to do with power.

The Power Lab has taught us several things about power:

- There is nothing inherently bad (or good) about it. The key issue is "How is it used?"
- It is unlikely that a group is totally powerless in any situation. A helpful perspective is to think in terms of ways to influence the situation.

- Feelings of powerlessness often come from untested assumptions. Information shared directly between groups "tests" assumptions and gives people real data to act on, thereby clarifying issues and increasing possibilities for cooperation. Too much energy is wasted acting on assumptions about what the "other side" is doing.

A group's effectiveness in problem solving can be enhanced by working with a grid perspective instead of an either/or perspective. "I'm right" does not always mean "you're wrong." If the assumption is that "I'm right" *and* "you're right," then an either/or perspective simply does not fit.

Either/Or Perspective: I'm right . . . . You're right

If the framework dealt with is a continuum as shown above, resolution of differences must take the direction of whoever is stronger or craftier. To the extent that one party wins, the other loses.

Grid Perspective

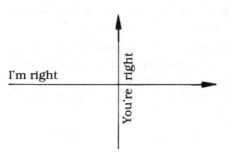

The grid framework allows for the probability that both parties are right. The resolution can be collaborative and can meet at least some of both parties' needs since the two viewpoints will likely converge at some point.

We learned about the grid approach when we were doing community-development training at the University of Minnesota. Sam had been working with community organization and organization development from a political-systems approach, trying to effect change in institutional practices. His co-worker, Mike, had been working in countercultural agencies and focused on individual life style and values. After several months of conflict, each accusing the other of not being very bright, they realized that it was possible to integrate both perspectives and generate alternatives for their work that were not available in an either/or framework. Their energy could then be directed toward answering questions such as "How is Sam right?" or "How is Mike right?" or "At what point do our approaches converge?"

An important factor in working with power issues is to keep in mind the differences between formal and informal power structures. "Formal power" refers to the influence people have because of their positions (elected officials, directors, chairpersons, and so forth). "Informal power" is influence that is not defined by an organizational chart; instead, it is determined by factors such as age, talkativeness, wealth, friends, and so forth and often has a greater impact on groups than the formal structure. It is also more difficult to identify.

One way to find out about a group's informal power structure is to ask three randomly selected group members the question "Who are the three most influential people in this group?" Their responses will yield a possible list of nine names. When those nine people are asked the same question, the possible twenty-seven names that result will include duplications. A rough idea of where the informal power lies can be established by counting the number of times each name appears.

A basic understanding of change, the importance of groups, and power provides a sound beginning for making change in any setting. Also, because everyone is involved in a group of some kind, the group provides a good setting in which to study how change happens, how decisions are made, and how power is used. Organizational-change efforts require working with groups, and effectiveness in groups is linked very closely to effectiveness in relation to issues.

REFERENCES

Alinsky, S. *Rules for radicals.* New York: Random House, 1971.

Oshry, B. Power and the Power Lab. In W.W. Burke (Ed.), *New technologies in organization development: 1.* San Diego, CA: University Associates, 1975.

Toffler, A. *Future shock.* New York: Random House, 1970.

RELATED READINGS

Alinsky, S. *Reveille for radicals.* New York: Vintage, 1969.

Bennis, W., Benne, K., & Chin, R. *The planning of change.* New York: Holt, Rinehart and Winston, 1969.

Christenson, J.A., & Robinson, J.W., Jr. (Eds.). *Community development in America.* Ames: Iowa State University Press, 1980.

Fessler, D.R. *Facilitating community change: A basic guide.* San Diego, CA: University Associates, 1976.

Harrington, M. *The other America.* New York: Macmillan, 1962.

Lippitt, G.L. *Visualizing change: Model building and the change process.* San Diego, CA: University Associates, 1973.

PART I

SELF-AWARENESS

A group is more effective in achieving its goals when its members make good use of their personal attributes. A conscious process of self-awareness on the part of individuals and groups makes them both more effective. By paying attention to our own patterns, values, strengths, and relationships, we are able to appreciate the actions and feelings of others. This awareness can help group members work with each other instead of against each other and can contribute to overall group effectiveness.

Chapter 2 describes a variety of leadership functions that contribute to group effectiveness. The process politician views leadership as a set of functions or roles that are shared by members of a group rather than as a position that one member occupies.

Chapter 3 suggests several ways to look at personal needs and group involvements. Being clear about our own values, strengths, and motivations can help us choose group activities in which we will be effective.

Chapter 4 focuses on the important role of ongoing support groups in helping to prevent the tendency toward burnout and loss of perspective that sometimes afflicts members of groups.

CHAPTER 2

THE PROCESS POLITICIAN

Process politicians increase group effectiveness by supporting the efforts of group members to influence the group. When group decisions are made in a way that both reflects and respects the needs of the members, the group itself has greater influence because its decisions have greater support. A group in which decisions are made and implemented by many members is usually stronger than one in which decisions are made and implemented by a few, with the group's role primarily one of approving decisions or recommendations from higher authorities such as executive committees. The secret of being effective as a process politician is to draw on the resources and abilities of all group members in order to come up with accurate understandings and effective actions in a variety of situations.

It is important to distinguish between being *effective* and being *efficient.* Modern-day society puts a high premium on efficiency (fast, cost-effective, product-oriented thinking). However, being effective change agents calls for a different approach, one that considers *goals,* or *what* the group is seeking to accomplish, as well as *process,* or *how* the group functions and how its members feel about their involvement. *The way in which decisions are made is just as important as the nature of the decisions themselves.*

It is the responsibility of process politicians to help their groups to be conscious of process concerns: to solicit ideas from many different sources, to help members express and deal with their feelings about their involvement in group concerns, to encourage their groups to explore alternatives before deciding on courses of action, and to assist members in making use of self-interest issues as they work together to accomplish their goals.

It is not necessary for anyone to have the title "process politician" to be able to act in that role. Sometimes it is effective for one member to function unobtrusively by calling the group's attention to its own processes. Another alternative is to have members share the functions of a process politician. It does not matter whether the function is performed by one person or by many; what does matter is that someone be concerned about how decisions are being made and how the group is functioning.

The best decisions are ones that take into account both long- and short-term effects and that many people have a part in formulating. The process politician helps bring ideas into the open by helping people understand the value of hearing many points of view. Two people can come up with a plan; but if two more are consulted, two additional points of view can be built into carrying out the agreed course of action. The planning process takes longer for four people than for just two, but the extra time required is well spent because better decisions are made; group members who feel listened to and included in decision making will invest more of their energy in helping the group implement its decisions than those who feel excluded, cut off, and powerless.

An important part of being an effective process politician is to deal with emotional as well as political realities. The process politician helps group members to consider people's feelings and to know that it is all right to do so within the context of a meeting. If one group member simply states that he or she is confused about what is going on and asks for help, it is easier for others to share their own feelings. One way to measure effectiveness in working with groups is to determine whether or not people need time to unwind after meetings. A group whose members can go home with a feeling of accomplishment and a clear sense of direction is more effective in that regard than a group whose members need two hours to unwind before they can sleep.

This does not mean that every group member needs to share the details of his or her most recent family spat. Such a revelation is not of concern to the group and is irrelevant to the business at hand. But a process politician's responsibility does include helping group members express feelings and reactions to issues under discussion and to the dynamics of the meeting itself.

The process politician can also assist a group by compiling ideas and concerns from different members so that the group can begin to develop action plans. It is important to remember that a process politician is primarily not a decision maker but rather a provider of assistance to help people make decisions on their own. Group members always know more about their own group, their problems, and their direction than any outsider possibly can. The process politician acknowledges the fact that expertise comes from life experiences as well as from formal training and that it cannot be measured by academic degrees alone. Groups that take advantage of the full expertise of their members have access to a broader range of information than those who rely primarily on a few members or on outside experts.

Another part of being a process politician involves enabling members to be aware of their own motivations and the motivation of other individuals or organizations. Part of group action depends on building action strategies that accept various motives and interests.

Effective group action relates to how well members' time and energies are utilized, how clearly members can express their expectations and work to fulfill them, and how flexible group decisions can be. A group can best succeed in reaching its goals when the expertise and individual qualities of its members are tapped. A process politician supports a group's growth and development in such a way that individual opinions are elicited and decisions are made that reflect the thinking of the majority of the group's members.

ROLES OF THE PROCESS POLITICIAN

A process politician's principal role is that of *change agent.* In addition, he or she may serve in any of several different roles, including that of *educator, advocate, fair witness,* or *idea generator.* All of these roles can be performed whether the process politician is a member of the group or an outside consultant, and all can be learned by group members who want to function more effectively.

Change Agent

Change agents—people who use their energy to work for change—can represent many different styles. A communist revolutionary who stands on the street corner and distributes leaflets is as much an agent for community change as a community organizer who teaches people to band together to achieve their mutual goals. Some change agents are *employed* to work for change, as in the case of consultants, counselors, and organization-development specialists; others are *volunteers,* as in the case of committee members, planning-council members, and block-club leaders.

Process politicians, paid or volunteer, are change agents by definition; they help group members become more capable of solving their own problems effectively. They also help people learn to be better leaders so that these leaders, in turn, can increase their groups' abilities to achieve goals. The particular change that process politicians work to bring about is more openness in decision-making processes and, thus, better decisions. For process politicians, the outcomes and decisions themselves are secondary to the process by which those outcomes and decisions are reached.

Sam was asked to be a consultant to the board of directors of a halfway house. His contract stated that he was to help the group work together better, without taking sides or advocating a particular direction or position on any issue.

Eileen was elected to serve on a citizen advisory committee to advise the city council on how to spend Community Development Block Grant funds. Since she was new to community-development and housing issues, she decided to make use of her expertise in process techniques while she became more familiar with the substance of the discussions. She volunteered to deal with decision-making openness.

Educator

A process politician sometimes functions as an educator by helping a group see itself more clearly or by consulting with individual members. The specific nature of this function varies with the situation.

Eileen was asked to teach decision-making skills and conflict-resolution techniques to a group of community leaders. She presented the leaders with a series of workshops designed to help them look at their own styles of participating in problem solving.

The educator does not have to be seen as a traditional teacher who stands in front of a group and lectures about theory. Instead, the process politician as educator uses a variety of teaching techniques, including small-group discussions, films, experiential-learning activities, and written materials. It is useful for a process politician to know some group-decision-making and personal-dynamics theory as a framework from which to operate, however. Also, knowledge of theory is much more useful if the process politician has experiences with which to relate such theory.

The process politician as educator demonstrates ways in which to obtain group consensus, advises group leaders on how to run successful meetings, and helps group members learn about resources and issues pertinent to the group.

Because the process politician may be in contact with many different people during any particular week, the opportunities for informal education and information sharing are also great.

> When someone calls Sam for advice in preparing a grant proposal and how to get it funded, Sam is aware of that request as an opportunity to teach some process-oriented skills as well. He may bring up the issue of self-interest or open participation in decisions as a way to increase awareness and to do some community education.

> Eileen, as chairperson of the planning council for her community, demonstrates styles of openness in discussing issues. She checks frequently during meetings to see whether anyone feels interrupted or misunderstood and encourages group members to express disagreements so that all points of view are taken into account.

Advocate

Occasionally a process politician is called on to be an advocate for a group. This function might include an activity such as speaking to a city-council subcommittee about the problems in the neighborhood or helping a next-door neighbor obtain needed medical care. Advocacy also might include taking public positions in support of open decision-making processes.

> We, as the authors of this book, are examples of process politicians as advocates for a particular position; the book was written to "sell" our ideas about the virtues of process and participation.

> Whenever we try to obtain funding for a project or proposal that interests us, we are acting as advocates for a certain point of view or a certain program. We do not take part in projects that we cannot advocate on a personal level.

The process politician as advocate can function as a group member, a consultant, or a staff person employed by the group or by a larger organization of which the group is a part. The advocacy techniques used for any of these positions can range from writing a letter to a city-planning commissioner to visiting the welfare office with a client/friend in need of help. The choice of techniques varies with the situation.

Fair Witness

Groups sometimes have difficulty in perceiving themselves accurately. When a group is so focused on its goals that the needs of its members and its internal dynamics are ignored, the fair-witness role of the process politician becomes important. The fair witness helps a group by providing a mirror through which members can take an objective look at themselves as they work. By stepping out of the task discussions, the fair witness can devote full attention to such matters as who is talking, who is not participating, body language, whether or not people are listening to each other, how decisions are being made, and so forth.

Group members can be free to become totally immersed in certain tasks, knowing that a fair witness is on the job to help the group function. A group can ask for fair-witness observations at any time during a meeting or at the close of a meeting. It is important that the fair witness try to express observations objectively, avoiding judgments about what has been seen. For example, the statement "I'm not sure Howard understood what Louise said" is more useful than the statement "Howard should listen better when Louise says something."

The fair-witness role can be performed by any member of a group or by a staff person. One useful way of incorporating this role into a group's life is to pass it around, each time requesting that a member with less interest in the subject under discussion be the fair witness. With time every member of a group can have an opportunity to be a fair witness, and the group's level of awareness about process issues can be increased.

Idea Generator

Sometimes a group becomes so involved with solving problems that it does not see all the available options. This situation often arises when conflict springs from an "either/or" approach to a problem. When this happens the process politician can serve as an idea generator who helps a group consider a variety of alternative solutions to a tough problem. Sometimes it is useful for the process politician to encourage the group to brainstorm different ideas without discussing or judging them. A group that uses only parliamentary procedure in its meetings may not be considering some good alternatives; when a motion is on the floor, the group's attention is limited to that idea. At this point a process politician as idea generator can provide assistance by suggesting that the group members try listing several options before starting the narrowing-down process of deciding what is to be done.

POWER

As suggested in Chapter 1, power is crucial to a group's effectiveness; it is an important element not only within the group itself, but also in the group's dealings with other groups and with larger organizations. *Power is the ability of an individual or a group to influence other individuals or groups.* This ability to influence reveals itself all the time, in positive, negative, and neutral ways. Although the idea of power dynamics often suggests stress and struggle, power itself, as emphasized previously, is amoral—neither good nor bad. Power can be used in positive or negative ways to achieve goals perceived as good or bad. It is sometimes difficult to determine how power is being used and whether it is working for or against the goals that have been set. The tendency of most people is to be suspicious about power until the specific situation is understood.

An organization elected a new board of directors, some of whom were new to the organization. They questioned many employees about various organizational issues in an effort to determine whether they were being given biased or objective information. They were hesitant to rely on any single source of information until they knew more about that particular employee. The new officers continued their questioning and asked the resource people to help in any way possible.

The process politician helps to increase people's awareness and effective use of power. Unless people acknowledge and use their own power, they are relinquishing it to others. Sometimes this circumstance is inevitable; sometimes it is a conscious choice. The important point is that *each individual must pay attention to the power that he or she has, the power that others have, the way in which he or she is using personal power, and the way in which his or her use of power is perceived by others.*

Power takes many forms: passive, assertive, formal, or informal. Personal power can take the shape of having money, having a dynamic personality, having permission to speak for a group, or knowing the right people. Group power can consist of having many members, being designated an "official" representative of a certain viewpoint, being successful, or having access to sources of information.

The board of directors of a community program had to decide whether to remain autonomous or to become a department of a major hospital so that the future funding of the program would be ensured. The motion to join the hospital was made and seconded, but no one seemed ready to vote. Finally, the chairperson asked for the opinion of one of the original board members, who had not yet commented. He spoke in favor of the motion, and the motion passed. It was the chairperson's assessment that there would have been no action without that individual's input.

It is especially important for the process politician to understand the dynamics of power so that he or she can help others realize their own power. One way in which an individual can determine his or her own personal power is by listing occasions during which he or she exerted influence, asking a friend to do the same, comparing the two lists, and discussing the effectiveness of the influence exerted on these occasions.

HOW TO MAKE THE MOST OF PERSONAL ENERGY

Process politicians are often under pressure. They help resolve conflicts and try to be "on top of things" most of the time. However, reality makes it obvious that all people make mistakes, change their minds, and have days when everything seems to go badly. Thus, the following "rules to live by" were developed to minimize hassles and to make the best use of personal energy. Periods of frustration can be more easily coped with when these "rules" are kept in mind.

1. *Go with the flow.* The key to going with the flow is to remember that life is lived in the here and now, each day at a time.

Yesterday can be relived only as a memory, and tomorrow can be experienced only in anticipation. Energy spent in worry about what has happened in the past or in anxiety about what might happen in the future is energy that could be used more effectively by making the most of the present moment.

2. *Trust your hunches.* Everyone can benefit from getting in touch with common sense and following what it dictates. This rule is helpful in getting through strategy sessions or conflict situations. It can be useful to express a hunch: "I don't know where this notion is coming from yet, but I have a hunch that we're missing the point." The other people involved can then help sort out the logic and examine whether or not the hunch is on target.

It is important not to hold back opinions because of fear of what others might think. Intuitive thinking in brainstorming sessions can be very useful and can spark creativity among group members.

3. *Learn from what you do.* Process politicians should learn personally from their activities. A correlation seems to exist between the degree of learning from involvements and the amount of personal energy available for use: The more a process politician keeps learning, the more energy he or she has.

The individual who suspects that he or she may have stopped learning from his or her work should answer the following questions: Am I listening carefully to what is going on around me? Am I talking too much? Am I bored? How can I learn more from my present involvements? Are my present involvements appropriate for me, or should I consider dropping some? Am I saying "no" enough?

It is certainly natural and normal to become bored, to change interests, and to want to move on to new areas of concern. Many group members lose their effectiveness after being in the same arena for more than a couple of years. All process politicians should regularly examine how much they are learning and whether they are losing effectiveness so that they can make any needed changes.

One way to keep learning is to consider every activity as a course of study. In a meeting one can study the ways in which groups operate; while cooking a meal one can study the use of spices. This approach to learning means remaining constantly aware of the variety of ways in which an experience can be viewed, with evaluation and learning happening all the time. Everyone becomes bored with activities that have been completely mastered; thus, seeking new activities generates opportunities to keep learning.

4. *Keep your life in balance.* Each of us needs time for family, work, socializing, and being alone. A feeling of being "off balance" is

usually attributable to giving too little attention to one of these areas of life. People differ in the amount of time needed for these concerns; but everyone needs time for contact with other human beings, for feeling challenged and productive, for having fun, and for contacting his or her inner self.

The "right" balance of time spent on these concerns varies from person to person and changes over time. Everyone should determine which needs he or she tends to shelve during busy periods and what type of personal balance should be consciously planned for and achieved.

By completing the following work sheet, you can obtain an account of your subjective awareness of the energy flow in your life. Such awareness can provide you with valuable information that can help you be more effective.

□

Energy-Account Work Sheet[1]

List below your *energy resources* (the things that give you energy) as well as your *energy depleters* (the things that take away your energy).

Energy Resources   **Energy Depleters**

List the times in your life when you have:

1. Gone with the flow (by not fretting about the past or worrying about the future).

---

[1]Developed by Betty Aldridge and Warren Sam Miller, Minneapolis, Minnesota. Used with permission.

2. Trusted your hunches.

3. Learned from an experience.

4. Done something to get or keep your life in balance.

List your own rules for getting the most out of your energy:

☐

TROUBLE SPOTS

Some pitfalls in working with groups deserve special attention. Working with groups is difficult enough when everything goes well; it is hoped by sharing the problems encountered by other process politicians, some potential hassles can be avoided.

1. One problem, which is not unique to process politicians, is a feeling of *helplessness* or impotence. This feeling is discussed in detail in Chapter 10.

2. *Bad timing* is another potential problem in group dynamics. Ideas of good intention are sometimes frustrated simply because of bad timing.

> A planning group had recently added several new members and elected new officers. Several veteran members were anxious to start the new year with some bold new activities and pushed for action. The new members, who still felt uncomfortable in the group, resisted the "pushiness" of the veterans. The veterans' ideas were soundly defeated until almost a year later, at which time they were unanimously approved.

Some people seem to have developed, by experience or by intuition, a better sense of timing than have others. A good rule of thumb is that an idea whose time has come is one that relates to a need felt by several members of a group. Before formally introducing an idea to a group, it can be presented to several individual members to determine whether its timing is appropriate. Otherwise, trusting hunches is useful in judging the timing.

3. *Distrust* can also be a problem. Process politicians whose self-interests are not clear to their groups will have difficulty establishing open communication. It is important that process politicians be clear, both with themselves and with others, about what their personal interests are. If a group's members doubt the intentions of the process politician, they will have trouble accepting him or her in that role.

For a group member or an outside consultant, a useful technique to initiate discussion when a group seems to be struggling with feelings of distrust is simply to say out loud that there appear to be suspicions and distrust within the group. Raising the issue publicly at a group meeting can be the first step in alleviating these concerns.

Issues of distrust, like hidden agendas or suspicions, are best dealt with during the course of a group's normal activities rather than during special workshops or seminars on trust. Although working with groups and communities is serious business, the process politician should not take himself or herself too seriously. The ability to laugh at oneself is the key to avoiding this problem. When a process politician makes a mistake or feels at a loss, the best course of action is to stop, invite the group to join in acknowledging the problem, and proceed by asking the group for help. Sam uses an eleventh commandment to help him keep perspective at times like this: "Don't sweat the small stuff." Recalling the commandment with a group is very helpful in putting everyone at ease and focusing on the important issues.

4. Another area of concern is *confidential information*. Because process politicians talk frequently about the need for open communications, group members tend to come to them with personal concerns regarding their groups or other members. To avoid the temptation of using such information to manipulate situations, the process politician should encourage group members to talk directly with each other. A good approach is to offer to help bring about a direct sharing of concerns between the two parties involved but to refuse to get caught in the middle.

5. Trouble is easily generated by acting on *assumptions* without verifying them. The members of a group can save time and frustration in action planning by first ascertaining what assumptions they are operating with and whether these assumptions are valid. Eileen's refrain for dealing with an assumption is "Check it out."

A process politician can be involved in a variety of activities and can assume several roles. Specific roles and activities depend on the situation as well as the personal concerns of the process politician. Therefore, an effective process politician is always clear about his or her motives and goals.

RELATED READINGS

Eddy, W.B., & Burke, W.W. (Eds.). *Behavioral science and the manager's role* (2nd ed.). San Diego, CA: University Associates, 1980.

Heinlein, R. *Stranger in a strange land.* New York: G.P. Putnam's Sons, 1961.

Lassey, W.R., & Fernandez, R.R. (Eds.). *Leadership and social change* (2nd ed.). San Diego, CA: University Associates, 1976.

Schaller, L.E. *The change agent.* New York: Abingdon Press, 1972.

Watzlawick, P., Weakland, J.H., & Fisch, R. *Change: Principles of problem formation and problem resolution.* New York: W.W. Norton, 1974.

CHAPTER 3

SELF-KNOWLEDGE

As discussed in Chapter 2, process politicians operate in a number of different roles; in fact, they are often required to switch roles numerous times during any particular day, depending on phone calls, meetings that are scheduled, or information appearing in the morning paper. In addition to external factors, they have their personal needs and private lives to which they must pay attention.

How can a process politician cope with the potentially confusing situation of wearing such a variety of hats? Where can a process politician find stability in the midst of so many roles? Is there any universal answer to these questions?

One answer is *self-acceptance.* Process politicians must recognize themselves as human beings with the capacity for achieving great successes—and great failures. They have emotions, needs, and limits. They change, learn, and interact with the environment constantly; and each of them needs to have a stable base from which to operate.

Because it is hard to find stability in the world outside oneself, it is important to look inward. The individual who knows and accepts who he or she is finds it much easier to know and accept other people for what they are. This principle is the same as that taught by Socrates to his students thousands of years ago: Know thyself. When a person has achieved self-knowledge—at as many different levels as possible—then he or she has a basis for deciding whether to change and, if so, in what direction.

After achieving self-knowledge, a person can progress to examining who he or she is in relation to others. Questions to ask oneself at this stage of development are the following: Are my beliefs and goals consistent within themselves? Are they consistent with what other people in my group or community are saying? What, if anything, can be done about any inconsistencies?

The 20th-century French novelist, Robbe-Grillet (1957), wrote a story in which he describes a field. First he stands inside the house and looks out of a jalousie window, and he presents one description. Then he moves outdoors and looks at the field from another physical perspective. He keeps moving around and describing what he sees. Each description is different.

This example illustrates an important reality: If a person stands in only one position, he or she has only one point of view.

One way to obtain a sense of perspective about oneself is to listen to "internal dialogue."

Someone called Eileen to invite her to a movie. She decided to go, but not before silently going through a series of considerations about whether she had time, whether she wanted to see that particular show, and whether she wanted to do something else that evening. Each question—and each answer—revealed something about her personality and her needs.

Internal dialogue includes both emotional and rational components. In working toward self-knowledge and self-acceptance, it is important to listen to both one's rational mind and one's intuition.

An important aspect of self-awareness is the ability to experience the timeless qualities of the universe by periodically "stopping the internal dialogue."[2] There are many ways to do this: by watching the sun set, by traveling, by meditating, by worshiping, or even by listening to music. Still another method involves getting in touch with oneself physically and trying to sense how the body changes with changing mental pictures. Everyone has ways of stopping the internal dialogue. It is a good idea to try listing one's own personal methods and then to ask a friend how he or she does it. Regardless of method, this type of activity renews energy, lends perspective to everyday problems, and helps achieve distance from such problems.

SELF-AWARENESS AS A WAY OF LIFE

To process politicians, self-awareness is a way of life. It is a key to understanding themselves and a bridge to understanding others.

The many approaches to self-awareness have been given different labels over the centuries. The philosophy of yoga, for example,

---

[2]Stopping the internal dialogue was reported by Castaneda (1972) as having been used by Don Juan, the Indian wise man, to describe the process of altering consciousness by shifting from rational thought (internal dialogue) to intuitive and subconscious ways of experiencing reality. For additional material on this subject, refer to the Consciousness section of the Recommended Readings in the Appendix.

teaches about the need to be detached from oneself so that one can see his or her life more clearly. Gestalt psychology helps an individual act out his or her internal dialogue so that it becomes more visible.

Another way to increase self-awareness is for an individual to examine his or her key dimensions of experience: sense, interpretations, feelings, intentions, and actions. Although these dimensions are always a part of each of us, they are not always within our awareness. Increasing that awareness becomes a way of knowing oneself better, becoming more conscious of personal identity, increasing choices about whether to change oneself, and increasing choices about self-disclosure.

The *senses* include sight, hearing, touch, taste, and smell. They provide raw data that tell what is happening in one's environment. They also document interpretations:

Sensory data: "John is tapping the table with his pencil."

Interpretation: "He must be nervous about the speech he is going to give."

Interpretations are thoughts, ideas, impressions, beliefs, opinions, evaluations, and assumptions. In short, they are all the different kinds of meanings that all of us create to help us understand ourselves, other people, and situations. The interpretations that an individual makes depend on the information provided by the senses; the thoughts that he or she already has; and the immediate feelings, needs, and desires that the individual brings to a situation.

Feelings are emotional responses that occur inside the body, although they may have outward signs. For example, when a person feels angry inside, the outward signs may be tense muscles, flushed skin, loud and rapid speech, and so forth. Feelings are important in any situation and serve several functions. They can alert a person to what is happening and can help that person understand his or her reactions to a situation. They also can help clarify personal expectations in a situation. (Some feelings are felt because of a difference between expectations and what is actually experienced.) But feelings can only serve these functions if one is aware of them.

Intentions can be anything from immediate desires in a situation, to objectives to be accomplished during the day, to long-range goals for several years or a lifetime. Generally, it is the short-term intentions that people have difficulty being aware of and disclosing to others.

Actions are behaviors—the way in which an individual speaks, listens, and moves. Often people are not aware of their actions. For example, a person's bodily posture, facial expressions, and vocal characteristics are actions that are obvious but not necessarily to that person. It is difficult to be aware of all one's actions because so much is happening at one time. Nevertheless, these actions become sensory data from which others make interpretations.

Of course, no one has total awareness of all these dimensions even part of the time. Self-awareness is a continuous process of discovery. One way to help foster this process is to use a model called the Awareness Wheel,[3] which represents the five dimensions of experience just discussed. It was designed to be easy to visualize as a reminder of all five dimensions.

---

[3]From S. Miller, E.W. Nunnally, and D.B. Wackman, *Talking Together,* Interpersonal Communication Programs, Inc., 1979. Used with permission.

One way to use the Awareness Wheel is to work around it step by step while considering a group situation such as the following:

I see a number of people gathering in the back of the room [sensing], and I think they might be working on an amendment to propose to the chair [interpreting]. I feel very concerned about what it might be [feeling], and I want to help if I can [intending]. So I join the group [acting].

Any dimension can be used as a starting point from which any or all other dimensions can be examined. An individual's awareness increases with the number of dimensions explored.

As mentioned previously, the process of self-awareness is never ending. All of us change constantly, according to the situations in which we find ourselves at any given moment. Life is in a constant state of flux, but we can adjust to its changing realities by being aware of what is happening within us at each moment.

As shown in the following example, self-awareness increases a process politician's effectiveness.

Eileen knows that she needs approval from the people around her. She has developed a style of leadership that builds on that need, rather than denies it. When working with a group, she encourages its members to contribute their ideas early so that the decisions she makes are more likely to reflect the group's viewpoints.

It is not important whether it is good or bad to need approval from others; what is important is recognizing personal needs and preferences as they are. With both personal and group matters, it is important to know the *actual* situation so that progress can be made toward the *desired* situation.

People who belong to decision-making groups may say that talking about personal feelings is not appropriate in that context. However, because self-awareness is the key to being an effective process politician, dealing with feelings is not only appropriate but necessary. If members of a group feel confused, but no one mentions these feelings, the confusion continues. If, on the other hand, one person expresses the confusion and asks for help, then the group can provide more information toward resolution. It is useful to keep in mind that people usually like to be asked for advice.

Eileen was working as a consultant to the chairperson of a board of directors. The chairperson was feeling worried about what might happen during an upcoming meeting at which a critical issue was to be discussed. Eileen encouraged her to let the group know about her anxiety as a way of taking responsibility for her feelings and as a way of letting others know that they, too, could express their feelings. The discussion went smoothly, and the group reached unanimity about the issue being considered.

Three individuals came to Sam recently and complained about their personal frustration as a result of their department manager's tendency to cut off discussion. Sam urged each of them to talk privately with the manager and to ask for help in dealing with their concerns. They suggested to the manager that more time be allowed for discussing issues, and their comments were welcomed.

PERSONAL POWER

Identifying "personal power" is an important part of the self-awareness process because process politicians are so intimately involved with power issues. The process politician should take time to examine his or her own responses to power, needs to exert influence, and interest in building a power base in order to gain an understanding of group struggles with those same concerns.

Wanting to exert power and influence is what being a change agent is all about: When an individual is unhappy with the way things are, he or she wants to exert power to make things better. Power, as defined earlier, is *the ability of an individual or group to influence other individuals or groups.*

Occasionally the following question is asked: "Why is it that I don't feel powerful, even though I know a lot of people who have power?" Part of the answer may have to do with self-awareness and recognition of the many ways in which such a person actually has exerted influence on others. Another part may deal with how successful or unsuccessful *others* see this person's efforts to influence decision-making processes. It may be that he or she has unrealistic goals and has trouble feeling influential unless all of these goals are accomplished. Or it may be that he or she, in fact, is not listened to because of an inability to use personal skills effectively.

Making the most of personal power can be viewed as figuring out ways to make the best use of oneself by answering the following questions: What are my strengths? What are my weaknesses? How can I use my strengths more effectively in working for what I believe in? How can I minimize my weak points or, better yet, turn them into strengths? How can I use my power so that it benefits others as well as myself?

Thus, a personal power base starts with self-knowledge and leads to the ability to help others effectively obtain what they want, which, in turn, results in greater personal power.

THE INDIVIDUAL

Now that the importance of self-knowledge has been established, the next step is to explore ways of developing such knowledge. It is not easy to pursue a self-awareness program; but there are some tools, such as the following activity, that can be useful in getting started. Completing this work sheet may help you increase your self-awareness, thereby increasing your personal power and developing your abilities as an effective process politician.

□

Self-Analysis Work Sheet

Part I: Who Am I?

Describe yourself to a perfect stranger by writing ten phrases that answer the question "Who am I?"

1.

2.

3.

4.

5.

6.

7.

8.

9.

10.

People often think of themselves in roles, such as those of teachers, parents, or secretaries. But people also possess knowledge, feelings, physical bodies, sets of values, and spiritual realities that shape who they are. Keeping this information in mind, review the ten descriptions you wrote and decide which of the phrases describe each of the following: *roles, inborn characteristics, personality qualities, skills,* and *other features.*

Part II: How Do Others See Me?

List ten phrases that other people might use to describe who you are.

1.

2.

3.

4.

5.

6.

7.

8.

9.

10.

Review Parts I and II and consider answers to these questions: In what ways are the two lists the same? In what ways are they different? Think about what you are learning about yourself.

Part III: The Chapters in My Life

Another way to look at who you are as a unique individual is to consider your life experiences and what you have learned about yourself from them. The experiences in a life usually group themselves into what can be called "natural chapters." For example, each of us experiences childhood, adolescence, being a student, changing jobs, and so forth. Think about the chapters in your life and list the five major ones at the top of the next page.

1.

2.

3.

4.

5.

How did one chapter lead into the next? Were there sharp breaks between chapters, or was there a flow from one to another? How long did each chapter last? What were the significant things that you learned while you were in each of the chapters? Can you predict what might be your next chapter? You have just identified some of your *developmental phases,* still another way of looking at who you are.

Part IV: My Skiils

Another part of you that is important to consider is skills. List the things that you can do well.

1.

2.

3.

4.

5.

Now consider what other people think you can do well. It is a good idea to ask some of your friends or family what they think of as your particular skills. Consider these evaluations and accept them; too often we overlook our skills. Also, think about what you want to learn to do better. Begin to find ways to improve your weaknesses and turn them into strengths.

Part V: My Personality Traits

Focusing on personality traits is also a way of finding out more about who you are. List the qualities that you possess—positive, negative, or neutral.

1.

2.

3.

4.

5.

6.

7.

8.

9.

10.

Now review the list and ask yourself the following questions: Which qualities are less used than others? Which are not well developed? Which are not shared sufficiently? In what ways do I stop myself from using those qualities? What could be good about sharing those qualities more? Which qualities am I in charge of? Which are in charge of me?

□

Knowing oneself is a first step. It is also important to take a look at personal motivations for actions. Each of us has developed a value system for determining what is important in life. These values form a framework for deciding what is right or wrong, how to spend time, and which goals to work toward achieving.

Two people were comparing opinions on how best to prepare for the future. One person was convinced that the most important factor in planning ahead was financial security. That person was investing in real estate and insurance policies. The other person was convinced that the most important thing to consider was physical health. That person jogged five miles every day, swam regularly, and ate natural foods.

Each of these people had developed a value system that reflected how he or she decided what was important in life. Neither set of values can be labeled "right" or "wrong"; each value system developed in response to the individual's unique life experiences.

The theory of *value clarification* offers specific tools that help identify individual values and the ways in which they change over time. This last point is critical as a reminder that we as human beings are in a constant state of growth and flux, necessitating continuous self-analysis of changing values and priorities.

The following activity deals with clarifying your own personal values about money, friends, time spent alone, issues, and priorities.

☐

Value-Clarification Work Sheet[4]

List twenty things that you like to do.

1.

2.

3.

4.

---

[4]Adapted by permission of A & W Publishers, Inc. from VALUES CLARIFICATION: A HANDBOOK OF PRACTICAL STRATEGIES FOR TEACHERS AND STUDENTS by Sidney B. Simon, Leland W. Howe, Howard Kirschenbaum. Copyright © 1972; Copyright © 1978 by Hart Publishing Company, Inc.

5.

6.

7.

8.

9.

10.

11.

12.

13.

14.

15.

16.

17.

18.

19.

20.

Now consider answers to the following questions: If you had to stop doing ten of these things, which would they be? Which of the ten things that you would continue doing are done alone? Which involve other people? Which cost more than three dollars to do? How often do you do your favorite things?

☐

Personal integrity is important in process politics. All of us hear about officials in conflict-of-interest disputes, activists who are discredited, and consultants who advocate their own beliefs. For the process politician, personal integrity is a key issue.

"Integrity," "personal ethics," and "morality" are terms that are seldom used these days. Often concepts of personal responsibility are de-emphasized in favor of such ideals as "efficiency" or "progress" or "cost effectiveness." However, effective process politics hinges on personal and professional integrity, even though the system in which the process politician operates may be amoral.

Are "pure" motives possible? Even if the answer is yes, the question may not be important. Integrity is simply a matter of being honest with oneself and straightforward with others.

Eileen was asked how to achieve effective citizen participation. She advocated that an independent "office of neighborhood participation" be set up as an advisory body of the city council. Recently, however, she argued *against* that position because she learned additional information that changed her mind. To maintain her integrity, she simply explains to others in a straightforward manner how she happened to change her viewpoint.

Sometimes it is difficult to determine when to compromise, when to capitulate, and when to advocate a position even more strongly. Maintaining personal integrity is not always easy, but it can be made easier by dealing honestly with doubts and uncertainties as they occur.

It is helpful to view the world as healthy and friendly. When uncertain about which course of action to follow, a useful approach is to ask oneself which course is consistent with one's original premise. If the proposal satisfies that initial review, then usually the question of personal integrity has been dealt with for now in such a way that feelings and opinions remain consistent and honest. This is an area of concern in which trusting one's hunches helps.

What makes one person become involved in a particular issue while others respond with apathy and indifference? The answer has to do with *self-interest—the most important concept in process politics.* To develop an understanding of this concept, try the following: Think about a group to which you belong. Ask a variety of people in that group why they are involved and what they derive from their involvement. Encourage people to be totally candid in their responses so that you can arrive at a better understanding of motivation. Then think about why you are involved and what your rewards are.

People often have a hard time answering questions about personal motivation. All of us have been programed to differentiate between "selfish" and "generous" activities, with certain connotations associated with these labels. "Selfishness" is considered bad; "generosity" is praised as a virtue.

Accepting these definitions and value judgments is not useful in process politics. Instead, the best way to deal with issues such as

motivation, participation, and effective group action is to understand and accept self-interest. *Self-interests are the factors that act as rewards for an individual or a group.* An individual's self-interest determines whether he or she stays involved with or leaves a particular situation.

People are motivated to do things to earn money and/or to gain some other kind of personal satisfaction. Sam uses the word "monergy" to express his incentives, indicating that his reward is sometimes cash, sometimes a gain in energy or in learning, and sometimes both. Any reward, whether in terms of money or energy or both, is adequate payment for an individual as long as it "feels" fair to that person.

A good way for each of us to look at motivation is in terms of this question: What am I being "paid"? The answers might include knowledge, new friends, social activity, or a feeling of accomplishment; the answers also might include frustration, anxiety, or burnout. To determine your own personal payoffs for your group involvements, complete the following activity.

☐

Activity/Payoff Analysis

List the group activities in which you are involved. Next to each, state what you truly feel is your payoff for that activity.

Activity	Payoff
_____	_____
_____	_____
_____	_____
_____	_____

☐

After completing the Activity/Payoff Analysis, it is a good idea to ask a friend to do the same, compare lists, and discuss the results. Completing this process helps to identify one's own self-interest factors.

Part of a process politician's responsibility is to get people involved and to keep them around. Understanding self-interest is the first step toward understanding people's motivations and reward systems. The succeeding steps of involving others will be dealt with later.

The notion of self-interest ties in with power and influence. A process politician who understands that everyone operates primarily as a result of self-interest concerns can make use of that principle in dealing with those in power, volunteers, and co-workers.

Dedication and pure altruism also play a role in process politics. However, anyone who claims to be acting solely on the basis of unselfish interests is fooling himself or herself and is likely to become fed up, frustrated, and ineffective. This is not to deny the importance of high principles but rather to point out that personal martyrdom wastes energy and promotes disillusionment and negativism. Sam uses the phrase "syndrome of the cynical social worker" to describe the behavior of professionals whose commitment to high ideals disguises their need for success, learning, and other self-interest payoffs. They develop cynical attitudes from denying these needs.

It is extremely important to reap personal benefits from involvement in group activities. Without such rewards it is ridiculous to expect anyone to stay involved for long.

An important dimension of being a process politician is the ability to disclose self-interest needs. Honestly stating one's motive or personal goal is helpful to everyone involved, makes the desired outcome more likely to happen, and clearly specifies one's personal agenda while encouraging others to do the same.

Everyone has so-called "selfish interests" for wanting to affect certain issues; these interests are not, in and of themselves, bad. In fact, the person who fails to acknowledge his or her own self-interests is being unfair, dishonest, and—in the long run—ineffective.

THE CONTEXTS IN WHICH WE LIVE

Developing self-awareness also involves developing knowledge of the context in which one lives. In many ways an individual *is* his or her relationships with others, and that person's interactions with other people and events shape who he or she is. No one exists in a vacuum.

Picture a car engine with the carburetor removed. That carburetor may be perfect, but it is nonfunctional as long as it is detached from the rest of the engine; the rest of the engine cannot work, either. The engine comprises the "context," and it helps to define what the carburetor is.

An individual can obtain a picture of his or her personal context by making a list of ten people from whom he or she has learned. These people are now a part of that individual; they helped to define who he or she is. Similarly, the challenge of figuring out how to make a group's "engine" work well starts with taking a look at how its members as individuals work in relation to their personal contexts.

One key to personal context is *feedback*. The term "feedback" has a particular meaning with regard to process politics and self-awareness. *Giving feedback is a way of helping another person to recognize his or her behavior. It is communication to a person (or a group) that gives that person information about his or her effects on others.* As a guided-missile system, feedback helps an individual keep behavior "on target" and thus better achieve goals.

- It *is descriptive* rather than evaluative. By describing his or her own reactions, the person giving feedback leaves the recipient free either to accept or to reject the feedback. Also, by avoiding evaluative language, the person giving feedback reduces the potential for defensive reactions from the recipient.
- It *is specific* rather than general. For example, telling a person that he or she is "dominating" is not as useful as saying "Just now you did not seem to be listening to what others said, and I felt forced to accept your arguments or face attack from you."
- It *takes into account the needs of both parties.* Feedback can be destructive when it fails to consider the needs of the recipient as well as those of the person giving feedback.
- It *is directed toward behavior over which the recipient has control.* People's frustrations are increased when they are confronted with shortcomings over which they have no control.
- It *is better elicited rather than imposed.* Feedback is more useful when the recipient requests that input.

Feedback is a way of giving help. It is a mechanism for individuals who want to learn how their behavior compares to their intentions. It is also a means for establishing one's identity and attempting to answer the question "Who am I?"

The basic principle about giving and receiving feedback is that when two people interact, each has some truth for the other to hear, whether it is reinforcing or critical. Unless all of us are willing to listen to what others tell us about our behavior, we cannot learn much about ourselves.

It is important to elicit feedback from others. A process politician who asks for criticism as well as positive comments sets an example while requesting personal learning opportunities.

Feedback can be elicited both formally and informally. Formal feedback occurs sometimes in the context of personal evaluations. Informal feedback can occur, for example, when acquaintances meet casually on the street or when an individual asks a close friend to evaluate his or her behavior in a specific situation. It can be helpful to set up situations to receive feedback about personal effectiveness. Before delivering a speech, for instance, it is a good idea to ask a friend to pay special attention to the style or manner of presentation so that the friend can make suggestions for improvement.

Feedback also can be incorporated into regular meetings. At the end of a meeting, for instance, a group facilitator can ask the group for responses to the following questions:

- What did you learn?
- What did you like about the meeting?
- What did you dislike about the meeting?

Individual responses are written on a chalkboard or newsprint but are not debated.

By giving as well as receiving feedback, all of us can learn about ourselves and our relationships with others. Giving feedback is an important part of helping each other to learn and to grow.

REACTIVE VERSUS PROACTIVE

With regard to one's personal context, one of two basic positions may be assumed. The *reactive* position involves reacting to issues that are presented by others.

Mary does not know what is expected of her in her role with the planning commission. The commission members accuse her of not being interested and not doing her job. Mary must *react* to these accusations.

The other position is termed a *proactive* one, in which the individual assuming this position initiates the issue and takes the offensive.

Mary realizes that she is underutilized in her work with the planning commission. She is not sure what else she could be doing for the commission and decides to request a meeting with the leadership to discuss her job and expectations of her position. Mary is in a *proactive* position in this case.

The proactive position is likely to result in positive action, thereby avoiding a situation in which the relationship between Mary and the group becomes polarized, complete with built-up resentments and accusations. For all of us, being proactive within the contexts in which we live and work is a way to work toward meeting our own self-interests. The proactive approach often results in shared problem solving and avoids unproductive blaming.

The process politician who operates from a firm base of self-knowledge—one who develops self-awareness and self-acceptance, makes the most of personal power, establishes personal integrity, understands the principles of self-interests, and assumes a proactive stance—is ready to learn how to survive the rigors of process politics without destroying personal energy or losing enthusiasm.

REFERENCES

Castaneda, C. *Journey to Ixtlan.* New York: Simon & Schuster, 1972.
Robbe-Grillet, A. *La jalousie.* Paris: Editions de Minuit, 1957.

RELATED READINGS

Bolles, R.N. *What color is your parachute?* (5th rev. ed.). Berkeley, CA: Ten Speed Press, 1979.
Dyer, W. *Pulling your own strings.* New York: T.Y. Crowell, 1978.
Raths, L., Harmin, M., & Simon, S. *Values and teaching.* Columbus: Charles E. Merrill, 1966.
Sheehy, G. *Passages: Predictable crises of adult life.* New York: E.P. Dutton, 1976.

CHAPTER 4

DEVELOPMENT OF A SUPPORT GROUP

Process politics is exhausting work. Many process politicians experience such serious burnout that they must drop out entirely to avoid damaging their mental or physical health. It is impossible to keep going forever at breakneck speeds. The problem is finding a way to avoid being ineffective or even counterproductive and instead to be an effective change agent who uses energy wisely. One solution is to make good use of the *relationships* found in a support group.

Support-group members may be family members, professional associates, next-door neighbors, or friends. They are the people who can be counted on to be there when needed. An individual's support-group members share some of his or her interests and values and are able to understand that person's feelings without receiving detailed explanations.

The members of a process politician's support group often serve an additional purpose: They act as consultants to such a person in his or her role as a process politician, thus making life less difficult and more rewarding. These people act as sounding boards, apprising the process politician of problems or inconsistencies in behavior of which he or she is unaware. They help such a person listen to valuable criticisms from others, and they provide shoulders to cry on.

Heterogeneous support groups consisting of people from a variety of concerns and experiences can be particularly valuable.

An individual can be explicit in asking people to be members of his or her "support group," or he or she can simply consider people as members without formally inviting them if their support is obvious. People are often flattered by requests to enter into such involvements and are usually eager to arrange the specific terms. The members themselves may never meet and need not even be acquainted with one another.

It may seem contrived to actually ask people to be personal supporters in view of the fact that primary support seems to come

naturally from family and friends. However, it is helpful to know that an explicit agreement has been reached regarding the specific nature of such relationships. In this way one can build mutually helpful relationships that enhance his or her personal life and effectiveness as a process politician.

Support-group members can help a process politician separate personal from group concerns. Process politicians need to be aware of the ways in which their emotions affect their group involvements. This awareness is hard to achieve because it is difficult to be objective about one's own behavior. A support person can provide valuable assistance in this regard by helping the process politician see more clearly what is happening.

Eileen and a co-worker were hired as consultants to a group in Eileen's neighborhood. She realized soon that her personal investment in the group was interfering with her ability to be an objective consultant. She asked her co-worker to help her distinguish her personal from her professional feelings as the two continued work on the consulting contract.

A support group can also help plan action strategies.

Sam asks his support group to be a sounding board for his ideas about group issues. Instead of waiting until the ideas have solidified, he calls on his supporters when his ideas are in the early stages of development. In this way he is more open to hearing criticism or suggestions. He often obtains new information that adds another dimension or changes his approach completely.

Eileen occasionally asks a member of her support group to preview a speech, review a letter, or suggest ways to deal with a difficult situation. The objectivity that a "third party" can bring to a situation can be the difference between success and frustration.

BUILDING A SUPPORT GROUP

Everyone has a circle of friends and other important people who provide support of one type or another. By completing the following activity, you can examine your own informal support group and begin thinking about ways to expand that group to make it work better.

☐

Support-Group Identification Form

List the people you go to when:

1. You have a problem.

2. You want companionship and nurturing.

3. You want to play.

4. You want good feedback.

Now review the list of names. How many times are names repeated? Is there any overlap at all? Think about why this might be the case. Do you prefer to maintain distinctions between your private and your working lives? What other patterns or surprises do you notice as you look at the list?

☐

Relationships are tied to self-interest concerns; we all choose to associate with certain people because we anticipate specific rewards from those contacts. This principle is mentioned to point out the practical nature of personal relationships, not to demystify the beauty of good friendships and other important relations.

Interpersonal relationships are based on interpersonal payoffs. The most satisfying and rewarding relationships are those in which a mutual give-and-take exists. All of us are teachers and learners in our important relationships; our acknowledgment of this fact helps us to grow personally and to enable others to grow as well. Completing the following activity will help you clarify the give-and-take in the relationships you share with those in your support group.

☐

Support-Group Relationship Analysis

List the people from whom you learn and what you learn from each of them.

Person   **What I Learn**

_____   _____

_____

Person   **What I Learn**

_____   _____

_____

_____   _____

_____

_____   _____

_____

_____   _____

_____

List the people whom you teach and what each of them learns from you.

Person   **What He or She Learns**

_____   _____

_____

_____   _____

_____

_____   _____

_____

Person	What He or She Learns
_____	_____
	_____
	_____
_____	_____
	_____

Are the people from whom you learn the same as the people whom you teach? What contributes to that situation? Think about the growing that you do in each of the relationships on your lists and the growing that you have helped foster in others. The most intense experiences with other people are those in which we grow together and learn about ourselves. These are not necessarily easy experiences because they involve taking risks, but they help us to become better people and better friends.

☐

In summary, the members of a process politician's support group not only respond in times of crisis related to issues concerning process politics; they also provide personal contacts. They supply the love and attention that process politicians need to maintain effectiveness.

RULES FOR RELATIONSHIPS

Every relationship has rules, and it is important that these rules be discussed and understood by those involved. In addition, strong support groups and healthy interactions in general can be built by observing the following two rules, which can be considered as adjuncts to the "rules to live by" presented in Chapter 2.

1. *Be honest with yourself and with others.* It is important to talk about what is happening in a relationship. If there are tensions in the air, ignoring the situation is not likely to make it go away. If a problem develops, the best way to handle it is to deal openly with the discomfort. Similarly, if an event occurs that results in excite-

ment or happiness, it is worthwhile to share those positive feelings. This principle applies in one-to-one situations as well as in dealings with groups.

Eileen's relationship with the chairperson of one of her groups has its ups and downs. They have philosophical disagreements that must be talked about honestly. They may not come to agreement, but they try to understand one another's beliefs and feelings.

Sam is pleased with the way that he and a partner have set up their consulting business. They build in positive rewards for themselves from their relationship. This positive tone enables them to work through difficulties from a sound foundation.

In the context of being honest about feelings, it is helpful to use "I" statements. For example, *"I felt* angry after the meeting because some issues were not resolved" is a statement that invites discussion. On the other hand, a statement such as *"You really made me angry* when you left things unresolved" sounds like an attack and is likely to shut off discussion or to provoke defensive arguing.

It is also helpful to pay attention during discussions to the nature of the exchanges. The individual who can pick up cues that trigger defensive responses as well as those that invite resolution is at a distinct advantage in interpersonal relationships. It can also be beneficial to examine one's responses to the phrases that other people use to raise issues or to discuss differences of opinion. To further assess and develop your own relationships, try the following: Ask your friends for their interpretations of the way in which you deal with your feelings. Ask them if it is hard to approach you about touchy subjects. Taking this risk can open up relationships and can help you to learn about yourself.

Another useful approach in dealing with others is to use behavior descriptions when expressing or working through feelings. For example, making a comment such as "When you raise your voice, I feel threatened" helps the other person to understand the situation.

At a meeting of city-council members and community residents, a leader from the community complimented the council for inviting residents to the discussion: "When you invited me here, I felt flattered and determined to do my best to have a fruitful session." This comment gave others positive energy and allowed the community leader to share good feelings. It also encouraged positive responses and mutual efforts to have a worthwhile meeting.

Being honest does not always mean telling people exactly what is thought of them or their ideas. It does mean expressing *personal* opinions or feelings clearly and tactfully. If negative feelings are dealt with the moment they arise, they are less likely to become serious problems later. Working together to resolve conflict can bring people closer, whereas not resolving conflicts can cause severe troubles and alienate people.

2. *Ask for what you want.* This rule is more complicated than it appears. *Asking* for what is desired necessitates *deciding* what is desired, *examining* the implications of that decision, and *taking the risk* of rejection of the request. However, desired changes in relationships are seldom achieved unless they are clearly stated.

This rule applies on a personal as well as a group level. For example, a group of friends who are trying to decide how to spend the evening could sit for hours while each person in turn says, "I don't care; I'll do whatever the rest of you want to do." In reality, it is unlikely that individual group members do not have preferences in most situations. But if these preferences are not voiced, the chances are slim that the group will act accordingly.

It is unrealistic for any of us to expect others to correctly guess our desires; we might wait endlessly for others to read our minds. This approach is not only fruitless; it is also detrimental to relationships. The end result might be resentment of what is perceived to be a lack of thoughtfulness on the part of the individual who is expected to guess correctly.

On a group or community level, as in personal situations, it is important for members to ask for what they want. Individual group members have relationships with the group in much the same way as two individuals relate to each other. Group goals are incorporated into bylaws or resolutions; personal goals or desires within that group context must also be addressed directly.

> One of the goals of a group to which Eileen belongs is to build group identity and to strengthen the ability of its members to influence their own lives. Within that framework Eileen would like to see activities and projects that get people together informally to have fun and to get to know each other.

COPING WITH STRESS

Being a process politician can become a strain on anyone. Sometimes it seems that there will never be enough hours in the day to finish

everything that needs to be done, and it is easy to become impatient with the slowness of bureaucratic or democratic machinery.

We all go through ups and downs. Unfortunately, though, the demands on a process politician do not take personal fluctuations into account.

One group leader was going through a difficult time recently. He was torn between his desire to spend time at home with his wife and family and his desire to honor his commitment to the group.

Honesty is the best response in such situations. If people are aware that an individual is under some stress in his or her personal life, they are better able to be sympathetic and understanding. It is not necessary to reveal the details of a personal problem or dilemma, but it is helpful to make people aware of one's life situation in general.

> All of us should draw on the resources of our support-group members when we feel that our energies are low. None of us can be on top of things all of the time. We need our co-workers, friends, and the other important people in our lives—as well as occasional vacations—to keep things in perspective so that we can accomplish our goals.

RELATED READINGS

Rogers, C. *On becoming a person.* Boston, MA: Houghton Mifflin, 1961.

Maslow, A. *Toward a psychology of being.* New York: D. Van Nostrand, 1962.

PART II

GROUP EFFECTIVENESS

Observing the ways in which change takes place through formal and informal action in groups can provide the process politician with a broader understanding of change dynamics. Part II presents a variety of practical suggestions for helping a group to be effective, whatever the issue. These ideas emphasize broad sharing of opinions as well as the participation of as many group members as possible.

Chapter 5 presents theoretical models of group functioning and suggestions about ways to conduct periodic checkups of a group's decision-making style and member satisfaction.

Chapter 6 introduces a step-by-step approach to planning a group's actions, beginning with identifying a focus and progressing to ways to set objectives and evaluate progress. The basic outline is applicable to any issue and is designed to help a group plan for success.

Specific ways to facilitate a group's decision-making process are identified in Chapter 7. These concepts and tools are designed primarily to promote the active involvement of all group members in arriving at decisions that will be carried out.

Chapter 8 acknowledges the informal activities that always are part of a group's life. Without behind-the-scenes conversations and thought, group decision making could be extremely time consuming.

Chapter 9 is about conflict. The subject of conflict is viewed from a positive perspective: Without diversity of opinion, a group would not be very interesting. A framework is provided for conflict management, including basic steps for constructive resolution.

Active people commonly experience the feeling of not knowing how to proceed or to be effective. Chapter 10 suggests ways to determine what to do when this feeling arises.

The real test of a group's effectiveness lies in its ability to influence other groups and collections of groups. Chapter 11 discusses institutional values as a key to understanding social change in larger contexts.

CHAPTER 5

HOW GROUPS OPERATE

Groups, like individuals, are growing organisms. They experience childhood, adolescence, and adulthood, complete with the emotional pains and joys of each phase.

In process politics *a group is defined as a collection of people who choose to interact around their common needs.* Group members share certain values and self-interests and work together to achieve their shared goals. Even small groups may also include subgroups, each of which has a life of its own. Groups include people who are working out their relationships with the group and with each of the subgroups.

It is helpful to have a basic understanding of the principles of group dynamics so that the struggles experienced by a group are more understandable. Knowledge of the ways in which groups work can enable a group's members to look objectively at their group's development and to celebrate its progress. For example, try the following: Think back to the last meeting that you attended. How would you rate your overall satisfaction with that experience? What factors contribute to your assessment?

The key point of this chapter is that groups can be observed and managed. Knowledge of group development and group process is essential background information that helps a process politician assess what is happening and how to make things happen better. Group dynamics is fascinating to learn about, especially since all of us are so directly affected by the groups around us and the decisions that they make.

The basic principle of group dynamics is that a group has both *task* and *maintenance* dimensions. Group members need to pay attention not only to accomplishing goals but also to the ways in which they interact. A group that focuses too heavily on tasks can have internal dissatisfaction, while a group that concentrates only on interpersonal relationships may end up accomplishing nothing else. Process politicians help groups balance task and maintenance concerns.

A group's growth and development take place both during and between meetings. Phone calls between meetings, for example, are bound to have some effect on the group's task and/or maintenance components. Regardless of the content of the conversations, relationships outside the group have a bearing on the group.

It is important to remember that groups are all composed of individuals with needs and interests of their own. These personal agendas call for as much attention as the group's shared needs and interests if the group is to be healthy.

PHASES OF GROUP DEVELOPMENT

No two groups are identical. They vary as much as the individuals who compose them. Conversely, all groups are similar in that they go through growth phases that have predictable characteristics. These phases parallel those of human development: dependence, counterdependence, and interdependence.[5] It is easiest to observe these phases in a group whose membership is steady over time; it is more difficult to distinguish the phases in groups with constantly shifting membership or goals.

---

[5]Adapted from CHANGING ORGANIZATIONS by W. Bennis. Copyright © 1966 McGraw-Hill. Used with the permission of McGraw-Hill Book Company.

During the *dependent* phase, group members depend on the leader(s) for direction and guidance. They are not yet sure why they are members, what they can contribute, or which roles they will assume within the group. They might accept tasks at the request of the chairperson, but generally they do not question that authority. The issue with which the individual group member is most concerned during this phase is inclusion: "How do I fit into this group? Am I a part?" This stage can be called the "childhood" of group development.

Soon, however, the group starts to encounter problems. A power struggle might develop, or a subgroup might attempt to railroad a decision. In any case the designated leader's authority is no longer accepted. This represents the *counterdependent* phase, during which the group members begin to assert themselves in the form of conflict with the person(s) in the leadership role(s). The primary issue for each member is influence: "Who is most influential in this group? How can I become more influential than I have been?" This stage is the "adolescence" of group development.

Interdependence, during which the members and the leader(s) work together in the process of decision making, is the mature phase of group development. It may take weeks or even years for a group with consistent membership to reach this phase; sometimes a group never achieves this maturity. Interdependence is characterized by open communication, accomplishments that the entire

group feels proud of, and successful recognition and management of conflict. The issues for each member during this phase involve communications and individual differences: "Do all the people in this group count? Has everyone had a chance to express an opinion?"

Development is difficult to monitor in many groups because membership changes frequently and new issues constantly arise. Nevertheless, it is possible to observe each of the phases with regard to a given issue.

The personal development of individual members in relation to the group is another indicator of how a group is functioning.

> Susan has begun to speak out at meetings—in opposition to members who have been around for a much longer time. Until recently she was more of a listener than an initiator. She has entered the "counterdependent" phase in relation to the group and is now investing more of herself; she has made a commitment to participate more fully.

As one member is experiencing counterdependence and challenging the leader(s), another may be relying on the leader(s) for instruction. A leader should recognize the diverse needs of individual members and of the group as a whole; in addition, he or she should help the other group members become aware of these dynamics by talking with them about their own growth phases.

A fundamental responsibility of process politicians is to help groups to grow and to see the phases of their own development. In order to determine where a group is going, it is essential to examine the group's position in relation to both task and maintenance functions within each of the developmental stages. For example, the process politician can point out the fact that as a group moves through counterdependence, the rebellion might not be primarily a personality issue involving the leader; instead, it might be a phenomenon directed at the *role* of leader. It is helpful for leaders to keep this in mind, too, and to avoid taking the rejection personally.

TOOLS FOR GROUP SELF-AWARENESS

It is essential for individuals to know who they are in order to grow. It is also important for groups to take time for periodic self-examination. This process enables members to identify what they like about the group's operation and what needs improvement. Many facets of group operation can be examined, and several "tools" are

available for use in helping group members to assess each of those facets.

1. Making use of a *fair witness* or *process observer* is appropriate, with either an outside person or a relatively disinterested group member serving as impartial observer for all or part of the group's meetings.

A personnel committee in one organization regularly invites a process observer to witness its meetings. This individual has the specific assignment of watching the interactions among group members. Observations are shared with the committee before adjournment, with discussion about ways in which the group could improve.

A process-observation report form can be used by the fair witness as an aid in watching for particular group behaviors and for giving feedback to group members. (See Figure 1.)

A group can decide for itself how to use the observations offered by the fair witness and may also ask for suggestions. If the discussion has been primarily among three members of the group, for instance, the fair witness might speculate that other people need additional background knowledge in order to participate more fully. Or the fair witness might suggest that the group talk about participation to determine whether the members would like to change or maintain the present pattern.

2. Another type of tool is called a *maintenance check*. A sample is provided in Figure 2; an entire sequence of five checks is included in the Appendix. A maintenance check can be used to diagnose a group's health in much the same way that a medical checkup detects danger signs in time to prevent anything more serious. A maximum of forty minutes is required for a group to complete a maintenance check; it is useful for a group to follow this procedure on a regular basis. Each member of the group spends ten minutes filling out the questionnaire. Then a sharing of responses and a total-group discussion follow. The questionnaire in each maintenance check focuses on a specific group function and is of value in determining the group's present phase of development.

Some groups use self-evaluation methods that combine personal interviews, written questionnaires, and group discussion. Others call in outside consultants to develop assessment tools specifically geared to their groups and the types of work that they do. Regardless of the format used by a group, *it is essential for group members to talk about how they are working together.*

Group _____ Date _____

Interpersonal-Communication Skills

    1. Expressing (verbal and nonverbal)

    2. Listening

    3. Responding

Communication Pattern

    4. Directionality (one to one, one to group, all through a leader)

    5. Content (cognitive, affective)

Leadership

    6. Major roles (record names of group members)

_____ Information processor	_____ Follower
_____ Coordinator	_____ Blocker
_____ Evaluator	_____ Recognition seeker
_____ Harmonizer	_____ Dominator
_____ Gatekeeper	_____ Avoider

Figure 1. Sample Process-Observation Report Form[6]

_____

[6]Adapted from J.W. Pfeiffer and J.E. Jones (Eds.), *A Handbook of Structured Experiences for Human Relations Training* (Vol. I, Rev.), University Associates, 1974.

7. Leadership style

_____ Democratic   _____ Autocratic   _____ Laissez faire

8. Response to leadership style

_____ Eager participation _____ Low commitment _____ Resistance
_____ Lack of enthusiasm _____ Holding back

Climate

9. Tone of feelings expressed during the meeting

10. Cohesiveness

Goals

11. Explicitness

12. Commitment to agreed-on goals

Situational Variables

13. Group size

14. Time limit

15. Physical facilities

Figure 1 (Continued).

Group Development

   16. State of development

   17. Rate of development

Observer Reaction

   18. Feelings experienced during the observation

   19. Feelings "here and now"

   20. Hunches, speculations, and ideas about the process observed

Figure 1 (Continued).

After a group has critically examined its operating styles, it can define its process goals. Members who have answered the questions "Who are we?" and "How do we function?" are then ready for the next questions: "What do we want to be?" and "How do we want to function?"

A university class decided to function in a shared-leadership style, rotating the responsibility for leading discussions among the class members and the faculty. All but three students attended regularly, but only about half of the group participated actively in discussion. After several weeks the class members concluded that they were comfortable with their informal style and with the sharing of leadership responsibilities, but that they were not happy about the uneven participation. The group made a commitment to consciously encourage everyone to express opinions. The faculty members agreed to contact the three students who had not been attending to invite them to return and to find out if some aspect of class operation was keeping them away.

Discussion about the ways in which decisions are made is best conducted in a total-group setting. No particular method can be advocated, however; each group needs to determine the style that works best for its members.

Step 1: Each group member silently reads the following questions.

1. What are acceptable and unacceptable ways of expressing different kinds of feelings in this group?
2. Are there any kinds of feelings for which there are no acceptable means of expression?
3. Do the members trust each other?
4. What are the characteristic ways in which less acceptable feelings show themselves, and how obstructive are these manifestations?
5. How much variance in individual styles of expressing feelings is tolerated?
6. How spontaneous, open, and direct are expressions of feelings?
7. Is the importance of the expression of feelings accepted?

Step 2: The group spends ten minutes in discussion as the individual members contribute answers to this question: In what ways have I seen some of these concerns raised in my experience in this group?

Step 3: Each group member completes the following questionnaire by circling the appropriate number on each line.

1. The way I express myself in this group is acceptable.

1	2	3	4	5
Never				Always

2. There are some feelings that I have trouble sharing in this group.

1	2	3	4	5
Never				Always

3. I feel trusted in this group.

1	2	3	4	5
Never				Always

4. I feel that unacceptable feelings in this group are obstructive.

1	2	3	4	5
Never				Always

Figure 2. Sample Maintenance Check[7]

---

[7]Adapted from a set of "maintenance checks" developed by David Goodlow for use at the Regional Training Center in Minneapolis, Minnesota, in 1972. The checks are drawn from materials developed in part by the Northwest Regional Educational Laboratory in Portland, Oregon. Used with permission. (This particular sample is shown here in simplified form; it appears in its entirety in the Appendix as Maintenance Check 3: Feelings.)

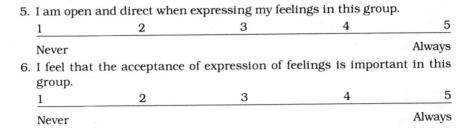

5. I am open and direct when expressing my feelings in this group.

1	2	3	4	5
Never				Always

6. I feel that the acceptance of expression of feelings is important in this group.

1	2	3	4	5
Never				Always

Step 4: The results of all members' questionnaires are recorded on a grid form that is posted for all to see. The group members spend fifteen minutes discussing the results, helping each other clarify and understand.

Figure 2 (Continued).

It may be useful for a group to define its participation expectations through process observation or maintenance checks.

The members of a board of directors were surveyed about their preferences regarding making decisions quickly as opposed to allowing maximum opportunity for discussion. The group agreed that it was important to consider all members' questions or opinions before coming to final votes. After this value was articulated, participation increased because all of the members knew that the others wanted their input.

A group that welcomes new members by telling them that there is group agreement on the importance of asking questions and speaking establishes positive expectations for the new members.

Another result of examining a group's interactions can be some decisions about the group's long-range or short-term goals. It is surprising how often groups can continue meeting without ever taking time to be sure that everyone shares an understanding of why the meetings take place. Many insights can be experienced when a group begins defining and clarifying why it exists and how it chooses to operate.

ROLES OF GROUP MEMBERS

Within every group, individual members are needed to perform specific functions. Someone has to take the responsibility for such tasks as bringing up new issues, notifying members about meetings, and providing background information when requested.

In group-dynamics literature, roles are discussed in relation to either *task* or *maintenance* functions. Task-related roles include those that help the group accomplish things; maintenance-related roles deal with the participation of group members. A list of commonly identified roles and their definitions follows.[8]

Task roles include:

- *Initiator:* Proposes tasks, goals, or actions; defines group problems; suggests procedures.

- *Information seeker:* Asks for factual clarification; requests facts pertinent to the discussion.

- *Opinion seeker:* Asks for clarification of the values pertinent to the topic under discussion; questions values involved in the alternative suggestions.

- *Informer:* Offers facts; gives expression of feelings; gives opinions.

- *Clarifier:* Interprets ideas or suggestions; defines terms; clarifies issues before the group; clears up confusion.

- *Summarizer:* Pulls together related ideas; restates suggestions; offers decisions or conclusions for the group to consider.

- *Reality tester:* Makes critical analyses of ideas; tests ideas against data to see if the ideas would work.

- *Orienter:* Defines the position of the group with respect to its goals; points to departures from agreed-on directions or goals; raises questions about the directions pursued in group discussions.

- *Follower:* Goes along with the movement of the group; passively accepts the ideas of others; serves as an audience in group discussion and decision making.

Maintenance roles include:

- *Harmonizer:* Attempts to reconcile disagreements; reduces tension; gets people to explore differences.

- *Gatekeeper:* Helps to keep communication channels open; facilitates the participation of others; suggests procedures that permit sharing remarks.

---

[8]Adapted with special permission from "What to Observe in a Group," by Edgar H. Schein, from *Reading Book* by Cyril R. Mill and Lawrence C. Porter, Editors, pp. 28-30. Copyright 1976 NTL Institute for Applied Behavioral Science.

- *Consensus taker:* Asks to see whether the group is nearing a decision; "sends up trial balloons" to test possible solutions.
- *Encourager:* Is friendly, warm, and responsive to others; indicates by facial expressions or remarks the acceptance of others' contributions.
- *Compromiser:* Offers compromises that yield status when his or her own ideas are involved in conflicts; modifies in the interest of group cohesion or growth.
- *Standard setter:* Expresses standards for the group to attempt to achieve; applies standards in evaluating the quality of group processes.

All of these roles are needed for a smoothly functioning, effective group. They may be performed by separate individuals or shared by group members at different points. A fair witness or process observer can watch a group meeting and give feedback regarding the roles that are operating, or the group members can spend time discussing which roles are easiest for them and which they need to build into their group.

If, for instance, a group does not include someone who assumes the role of "summarizer," then it is helpful to assign someone to that role or to remind members to speak up when it is felt that a summary is needed.

Dysfunctional roles also exist. Behaviors such as dominating, blocking, seeking recognition, avoiding issues, being aggressive, or distracting are disruptive to a group. Although it is not easy to confront someone about dysfunctional behavior, it is important not to ignore obvious disrupters. As discussed previously, "I" statements are helpful in this type of situation.

One member of a particular group regularly monopolizes the discussion, and other group members tune him out. The chairperson deals with the situation by saying, "I'm eager to get back to the issue that's on the table now. Would you like to request any specific action from the group at this time, Jon?" Such a statement usually enables the group to return to business.

Group members share the responsibility for dealing with disruptive members. Statements such as "I'd like to hear what others have to say" can subdue some members so that diverse opinions can be heard and discussed. The use of discretion is advised in deciding whether to confront someone in public or in private. Personal attacks are nonproductive, whereas sharing personal reactions can be helpful to the whole group.

LEADERSHIP

When the members of a group identify their leader, they usually name the person in the formal leadership position. However, if they look more broadly at influence and respect within the group, additional names come up.

A leader is any group participant who helps the group to achieve its goals. The distinguishing factor is not the number of ideas that a person generates or how loudly these ideas are expressed; rather it is the extent to which those ideas help to focus the group's energy toward a goal.

Just as formal and informal types of power exist within a group, so do formal and informal types of leadership. Some of the most influential people in any group are those without any official title, whereas some of the people with titles exert very little influence. The concept of leadership hinges on interpersonal relationships within the group. As relationships and issues change, so does leadership.

It is useful to think of leadership as a continuum between *laissez-faire* and *autocratic* styles.[9] The term "laissez faire" means noninterference, or essentially the policy of allowing others to do as they please. A laissez-faire leadership style emphasizes individuality and resists structuring the group to focus on either task or maintenance functions. Whether intentionally or by default, laissez-faire leaders encourage group members to do whatever they like.

> Susan was elected chairperson of a new group but felt unsure of herself as a group leader. As a result she hesitated to assert herself and tried to avoid making mistakes. The group members spent much time chatting with each other, and little was accomplished. Eventually members began dropping out.

In contrast, the autocratic leader forces the group to get the job done, whether that job consists of achieving task goals or working on maintenance goals. The autocratic leader considers open participation to be inefficient and only permits comments related to the tasks at hand. Members' feelings are unimportant and irrelevant in the eyes of an autocratic leader.

> John called the meeting to order. The secretary reviewed the minutes, and a vote was requested. John asked the next person

---

[9]Adapted from "An Experimental Study of Leadership and Group Life," by Ronald Lippitt and Ralph K. White, published in *Readings in Social Psychology* by Henry Holt and Company, Inc. Copyright 1958 by Ronald Lippitt and Ralph K. White. Used with permission.

on the agenda to present the committee's recommendation. The recommendation was given in the form of a motion, and the vote was taken. No "irrelevant" remarks were permitted; when such comments were made, John immediately ruled them out of order. The members went home feeling frustrated and ignored. They had many unanswered questions about what happened at the meeting and why they had been there.

Both styles of leadership are useful, but a "good" leader combines both styles. This middle-ground approach is called the *democratic* style of leadership.

Although the democratic style generally works best, certain circumstances may call for more "hard-nosed" or more easygoing styles. A forceful, autocratic style gets action; but a group can benefit from struggling to find direction, and that benefit is lost with an autocratic style. There is no "right" style of leadership; what is right is what helps the group to achieve its goals, one at a time.

Several tools and exercises are available for groups to use in analyzing their leadership needs and styles. Groups should talk about leadership and find ways to increase the leadership skills of their members.

Some groups function without a designated leader; they may rotate that responsibility, or they may deny the need for having a leader at all. However, every group has leadership, whether officially designated or not. Certain people exert more influence on group decisions than do others; and, unless this fact is recognized, a group that tries to function as a collective may be operating with blinders on.

How can one become a better leader? A first step is to become familiar with the roles identified earlier in this chapter. To be an effective leader, an individual must be able to function in a variety of roles as task and maintenance needs unfold. One's personal support group can be of value in helping to develop abilities in new roles.

DECISION MAKING

Process politicians help group members to become effective decision makers. Anyone who wishes to become more effective in this respect must first understand what constitutes a "good" decision. To be considered "good," a group decision must meet the following criteria:

- It must be carried out.
- It must take both facts and feelings into account.
- It must be understood by all members to have the same meaning.
- It must take self-interest principles into consideration.
- It must be derived from input from those to be affected.
- It must have few harmful consequences.
- It must make sense to everyone involved.

A group can reach good decisions through the use of any of a number of different techniques. Some groups operate most satisfactorily by using *Robert's Rules of Order*. Others combine majority vote and free-flowing group discussion. In some groups the formal leaders make decisions for others to implement, while in other groups decisions are made by consensus.

The important point is that *the group must consciously decide how to make decisions.* For instance, unless the members are able to openly discuss how comfortable they are with parliamentary procedure, they may never get a chance to voice their confusion or their preference for a more loosely structured procedure. There are no fixed rules regarding the way in which decisions must be made; the final choice rests with the group.

Some people may find that the most comfortable procedure in small groups is decision making by consensus. *Consensus is decision making that takes all members' personal opinions into account and results in a decision that all members can live with.* All members may not be totally happy with the outcome; but they have agreed that they can abide by it, and they feel their opinions were listened to and taken seriously.

Large groups have difficulty obtaining consensus without professional facilitation. Techniques to ensure full participation in a large-group setting range from allowing time for small-group caucusing to allowing each member to spend no more than one minute expressing a personal viewpoint. The process politician assists by calling attention to a group's options for reaching a particular decision, suggesting that the decision be (1) tabled, (2) divided into parts, (3) handled by committee and brought back in the form of a recommendation, or (4) left unresolved for the time being. The process politician can also remind the group to consider the nature of the decision and what approach would be most helpful in a particular situation.

Whatever approach is taken, encouraging the group to evaluate its results and decision-making styles is always a good idea, both as a preventive measure and as a way to remedy problems.

CONFLICT

Conflict is a sign of being alive; it is inevitable. Groups whose members argue stand a better chance of being able to come to good decisions than do groups whose members disagree with what is happening but keep their opinions to themselves. A group's leadership can solicit dissenting views and support the ideas of members as they work through both issues and process-oriented conflicts.

The way in which an individual responds to conflict depends on the situation and on his or her personality. The important point to remember is that conflict can be managed, resolved, and learned from—as further developed in Chapter 9.

MOTIVATION

People often ask how they can motivate their groups. The question of motivation is one of self-interest. People are "motivated" when they are deriving what they want from given situations. On the other hand, when people drop out of a group, they often do so because they are not getting what they expected.

The process politician helps people to identify their personal self-interests in regard to their particular groups. In addition, he or she tries to help both individuals and groups get what they want. The key is to help people to accept the idea that personal rewards are allowed and then to help them pursue their own payoffs.

■

Many fascinating developments happen in a group's life. Completing regular maintenance checks is essential to group effectiveness, in much the same way as self-awareness and feedback are essential to the individual. Group dynamics can be an exciting field of study for the process politician who helps a group to grow, to choose the styles of leadership and decision making that best suit its needs, and to understand its own internal workings.

RELATED READINGS

Argyris, C. Increasing leadership effectiveness. New York: Wiley-Interscience, 1976.

Blake, R.R., & Mouton, J.S. Corporate excellence through grid organization development. Houston, TX: Gulf, 1968.

Johnson, D.W., & Johnson, F.P. Joining together: Group theory and group skills. Englewood Cliffs, NJ: Prentice Hall, 1975.

Lippitt, G., & Seashore, E. The leader and group effectiveness. New York: Association Press, 1962.

Lippitt, R., Watson, J., & Westley, B. Dynamics of planned change: A comparative study of principles and techniques. New York: Harcourt Brace Jovanovich, 1958.

CHAPTER 6

PLANNING FOR ACTION

Process politics helps to manage change by developing steps for achieving long-range goals. Learning to deal with change is important for groups because they themselves are always changing. Even those individuals who resist change attempt to manage it in a way that suits their particular needs.

Action planning helps a group to find effective solutions to agreed-on problems. Through planning, group needs and personal philosophies can be translated into actions to which the group has a commitment. Group members share and discuss their perceptions in a way that promotes success in working together.

THE RATIONALE FOR PLANNING

Planning is done all the time by professional planners. There is always a need for coordinated planning and impact studies in every area of group activity as well as in such major areas of societal concern as health care, housing, and economic development. In addition, there is a great need for citizen input into planning activities.

A process politician looks for ways to assist a group in making its concerns known beyond the group itself to those individuals who are able to affect the group's interests. This assistance can be of benefit to group members by providing them with broader perspectives on their issues and a greater interest in the planning outcomes.

Effective planning makes it possible to get the job done in a way that makes group members feel productive and successful. The planner role can be shared, assigned to one person in a group, or handled by employed staff. In a sense planners function as cheerleaders, encouraging a group to applaud itself when it has achieved an objective, however small. They do this by working with groups to develop action plans.

An action plan becomes a road map for a group or organization to follow as it moves from where it is to where it wants to go. An action plan that is useful is one with flexibility for detours en route, with opportunities for stopping for maintenance work, and with realistic goals. Action planning makes it easy for a group to identify its successes and failures and to learn from them.

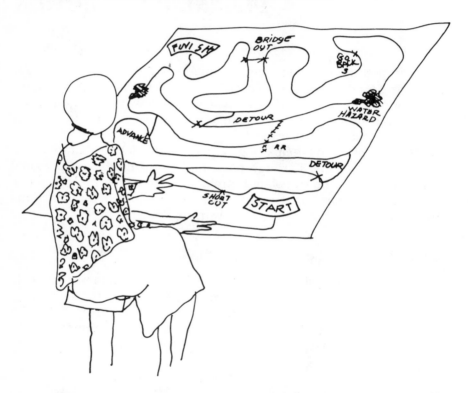

STEPS FOR DEVELOPING ACTION PLANS

1. *Determine the group's focus.* The first step in planning for action is to focus a group's energy. This may have been done prior to the group's first meeting; on the other hand, if there is no clear direction for the group when it first meets, that group must then establish its reason for being.

Almost any group can list more concerns than it has resources to work with; thus, it is important to limit the group's scope. One way in which a group can accomplish this is to require each of its members to list priorities for the group.

A newly formed advisory board had its first meeting. The chairperson started by sharing some of his interests in being involved with this new group. He then invited all people in the room, including spectators and employed staff, to offer their individual thoughts on the direction that the group might take during the coming year. The result was a long list that included everyone's ideas.

After a list of individual concerns has been developed, the group members can look for areas of agreement and select general priority themes for action.

2. *Determine the group's concerns.* After the group has identified its priorities, it can identify specific concerns related to those priorities. This process involves making contact with individuals, groups, or organizations to determine what is already being done to deal with the group's primary focus. If a group represents others or will attempt to influence some action beyond the group, its members should determine what others think about the group's activities and plans. If the group is a community group, for example, its members should determine the interests of others in the community because the group will need the support of such people in implementing its plans.

The members of a community group decided that the group would concentrate on dealing with the concerns of renters in the neighborhood. Many group members were renters themselves and were personally aware of the difficulties in dealing with absentee owners and discriminatory rental policies. All of the members met, shared their knowledge of the situation, and then divided responsibilities for arriving at a more complete assessment of renters' concerns by contacting community organizers, tenants' rights groups, and other individuals who were not in the group but who could provide additional information.

A group may obtain access to the opinions of nonmembers in several different ways. One way is to invite nonmembers to a group meeting to discuss all ideas related to the issue at hand. If this procedure is followed, it is important to remember that although the nonmembers' ideas or concerns already may have been expressed by members during past group meetings, the nonmembers are not aware of this fact. The time spent by a nonmember to think about group-related concerns and then to express ideas deserves appreciation. Thus, responses such as "Yes, we already thought of that and it doesn't work" should be avoided.

Another way to gain access to the opinions of nonmembers is to have each member of the group talk to five people who are not members. These people may also be asked to fill out a questionnaire. In some instances, however, it is easier to obtain responses by asking questions face to face rather than by using a written format. In general, a simple survey with one or two specific questions is more productive than a complicated form with many questions.

The workers at a community mental-health center had a booth at a neighborhood fair. They surveyed neighborhood residents by offering "a penny for your thoughts." Each person who completed the center's questionnaire by stating what other people in the neighborhood seemed most concerned about was given a penny. The result was a thorough (although unscientific) random survey.

Sometimes a more elaborate survey is necessary. A poll of scientifically selected people yields more dependable, representative information about the opinions of others but can be difficult and expensive to compute. Many groups and organizations employ professional pollsters to conduct such polls. Previous studies of the same or similar issues, political parties and candidates, or university departments may also be helpful in completing a needs assessment. Another idea is to arrange for students to receive credit for doing basic research and polling.

To obtain the best possible information about the attitudes of nongroup members, a variety of data should be collected from a variety of sources—including information from groups or agencies that may not support the efforts of the group collecting the data.

The members of a state agency started their needs assessment by visiting a sampling of communities in the state. They talked with various people and listened to their perceptions. In the process of listening, they gathered names of key individuals and organizations who were important to contact. Then they proceeded to contact each of those key people for their comments and advice.

The intended result of a needs assessment is that the members of a group develop a broad understanding of the problems they want to solve, the barriers they might encounter, and the general direction they wish to pursue.

3. *Write a problem statement.* A good problem statement grows naturally from the needs-assessment process just described. It summarizes the concerns that have been expressed by nonmembers as well as members, identifies particular symptoms, and provides a starting point for moving toward solutions.

A good problem statement is also specific. It deals with one issue only. If several problems are to be dealt with, several problem statements are needed. Ineffective planning stems from unclear statements about the problem with which the group is dealing. For example, the following is an unclear problem statement: Members of the group are frustrated. Although this statement may be true, it says little about the precise nature of the problem. Who is frustrated—all members or just a certain few? What are they frustrated about? What is the result of their frustration? When does their frustration occur? Who is bothered by the frustration?

Without answers to questions like these, eventually group members can find themselves working at cross-purposes. Spending time formulating a problem statement may be perceived as a nuisance when the members would rather work on solutions to the problem; however, unless all members share an understanding of the exact problem being dealt with, the group could end up wasting a considerable amount of time.

The process politician can assist a group in developing problem statements. Asking questions in the following format can be valuable:

- What is the nature of the problem?
- Who is affected?
- What is causing the problem?

Although there might be other aspects of the problem, the above format can be a beginning. This information may be obtained by using a general discussion or a questionnaire or through individual contacts.

After the group has analyzed its general statement in more specific terms, it becomes easier to see the many aspects of the problem. It is then possible to write a clear, meaningful problem statement such as the following:

> During the past several months, some members have felt frustrated with the internal mechanics of meetings. The long-time members are tired of having to repeat things for those who do not attend regularly. The new members are confused about the group's purpose and do not feel a part of the group's decisions. All members are uncomfortable with the absence of group discussion before decisions are made.

4. *Develop group goals.* After a problem statement has been developed, the group can move on to developing goals for action. Problem statements describe a situation as it is; goals describe it as those involved would like it to be.

Problem statement:	I am tired of the cold winter.
Goal:	To go to Florida next month.
Problem statement:	There is always garbage in the alley.
Goal:	To determine a way to keep the alley clean.

Establishing a goal is easy if the problem statement is clearly written. It is important to involve the total group in determining the goal. Such involvement builds group commitment to follow through later.

> Betty agreed to take responsibility for helping her group with its goals. The problem identified by the group was the absence of activities for teens, despite the fact that repeated requests for such activities had been made by both teen-agers and parents. At a meeting of the full group, there was open discussion addressing the problem. It was decided that the group would sponsor two evening events during the year and three weekend events to be developed with the assistance of interested teens.

The goal provides a specific direction for the group but does not include every detail regarding how to achieve the goal. Although it establishes a time guideline, the extent of activity, and the potential participants in the process of goal achievement, it allows for considerable flexibility.

Essentially, *a goal is a statement of a desired outcome.* In addition, a good goal statement is:

- *Clear.* The group members understand the goal and can explain it to other people.
- *Acceptable to group members.* Not only do the group members understand the goal; they also support the statement and will work toward achieving the desired results.
- *Flexible.* The goal is not so rigid that it cannot be modified as new developments occur either within the group itself or in the surrounding environment.
- *Long range.* A useful goal statement describes the end result of a group's efforts. It provides a sense of direction without locking the group into specific action steps.
- *Measurable.* It contains quantifiable elements that enable the group to gauge its success or failure.

Goals can be applied to either task or maintenance functions. For example, a group might establish a *task* goal to develop and submit a design for a new product line; or it might establish a *maintenance* goal to increase the level of participation at meetings over the next three months. Both types of goals are important in building active, cohesive groups.

5. *Set action steps.* After a group's members have agreed on goals, they are ready to work with individual objectives. *Objectives are statements of results that are achievable in short amounts of time.* They are the building blocks that enable a group to move toward its goals. The terms "strategy" and "action step" are sometimes used to mean the same as "objective."

Brainstorming can be very helpful in beginning to set objectives or specific action steps. For example, Sam assembled a group of associates who were interested in taking a trip. He wrote the goal statement, "To go on a trip at the end of next month," on a large sheet of paper and posted it for the group. He then asked the members of the group to list everything they needed to do in order to accomplish the goal. Anything was considered legitimate at this stage.

Brainstorming has one major purpose: to generate many different ideas in a short time. Creativity should be encouraged, and no discussion of individual ideas should be permitted until all members have had a chance to express themselves. The process politician can remind members of the purposes of brainstorming and ask members not to evaluate or categorize items until the brainstorming has been completed. In the case of the trip planned by Sam and his associates, the list of what needed to be done before the trip included many different items. Some were funny; most were very practical; others were puzzling and required further explanation.

The next step in establishing objectives is to review the items derived from brainstorming and ensure that everyone understands each item. The process politician can keep people on track during this procedure. It is important for the group to reach a consensus regarding items that are most relevant to achieving the goal. Any items that would not contribute toward achieving the goal can be eliminated at this point.

The list of "things to be done" for Sam's trip included the following:

1. Have each person state the amount of money that he or she can afford to spend on the trip.
2. Determine the approximate cost of the trip.
3. Find out whether the traveling companions want to make stops along the way.
4. Have the van tuned up.
5. Line up some substitute travelers in case anyone in the original group has to cancel.
6. Figure out what people should bring to minimize the costs of food and lodging.

The objectives were arranged in priority order, someone was assigned to each task, and a deadline date for each activity was established. Sam agreed to be the contact person.

Establishing group objectives is sometimes a long process. Goal and problem statements may be complex and may present several courses of action to be followed. There are no magic formulas for dealing with such complexities, but open discussion is useful when working toward a compromise solution. During the course of such discussion, consideration should be given to the feasibility of proposed action steps: Will the energy required to do the task yield commensurate results? Will the proposed objectives actually help to accomplish the goal? Will the group members invest their time in the project? No action can work unless the members are willing to take responsibility for seeing it through. Personal commitments are needed, and backup help should be available.

A good objective states:

- *What will be done.* When an objective is as precise as possible, the chances are greater that everyone will understand what to expect and what the outcome will be.
- *When it will be done.* A time deadline is a good accountability mechanism and provides a framework for the responsible group member.
- *Who will do it.* At least one person should be connected with each objective. The chairperson may either ask for volunteers or request that a particular person assume the responsibility.
- *What backup resources are available.* Some discussion about where to find additional information should be included.

Group leaders often end up carrying the bulk of the responsibility for their groups. By developing objectives that are of man-

ageable size, the members can divide responsibility more readily. A "group project" that is handled by only one or two members does not actually represent a group effort.

When members feel that their opinions are worthwhile and welcome, the group objectives will be implemented.

6. *Assess group progress.* Groups, like individuals, need to periodically engage in self-analysis. A group can only grow by examining what it has done, how its members feel about what has been done, and what has changed. It is through this same process of analysis that group members increase their knowledge of group dynamics.

The process of translating experience into something learned is called evaluation. *Evaluation is the assessment of the ways in which goals and objectives are implemented and the effectiveness of those processes.* When a group's planning results in clear goals and specific objectives, evaluation can be easy.

"Evaluation" is a term that sounds complicated and uninteresting. It is helpful to think of evaluation as a way of life rather than as a series of charts, statistics, and calculations. To evaluate a group's progress means to consider answers to questions such as these: How do the members feel about what happened? What exactly did happen? Why did the meeting go so well (or so poorly)? How satisfied is each member with the group's work? What has been learned?

The key to evaluation is to talk about what is happening. After a group's members have determined how they feel about the group's progress, they can decide what they want to do next. If no change is needed in the originally adopted goals and objectives, the group can then implement its action plan.

Evaluation occurs both formally and informally. It occurs, for example, when a group discusses its own decision-making processes, when a process observer shares observations, or when there is a structured discussion about how the group is progressing. The goal of evaluation is to learn what went right, what went wrong, and how to proceed.

After evaluation a group's original action plans often require modification. Conditions change, people change, and estimates of available funds may turn out to be wrong. Evaluation gives everyone a chance to revise plans to reflect new information or changing environments.

For example, in planning their trip, Sam and his associates saved themselves some energy by evaluating their situation. The original summary of their action plan was as follows:

Problem	→ Objective 1 →	Objective 2 →	Objective 3	→	Goal
"We're tired of this cold winter."	Find out how much each person can spend.	Find out how much the trip will cost.	Decide where to stop and whom and what to see.		Get to a warmer destination.

The four people making the trip found that they could spend a total of $225 on gas and travel expenses (Objective 1) and that a direct route would cost $220 (Objective 2). The small remaining sum of $5 greatly limited the leeway they had in dealing with Objective 3. Thus, they knew that they had to revise their original plan so that it would be more realistic.

The revision could be accomplished in a number of different ways. They could ask another person to go along; they could generate some financial assistance; or they could decide to take the direct route. The solution in this case was to add two new objectives:

Problem ——→ Objective 1 ——→ Objective 2 ——→ Objective 3 ——————→ Goal

Objective 2a: →Objective 2b:

Objective 2a:	Objective 2b:
Find another person to go on the trip.	Explore ways to have expenses subsidized.

The goal remained the same in this instance, but sometimes it is appropriate to alter the goal to be more in line with new information. Sometimes it is necessary to abandon a goal entirely; if a situation does not work out as expected, it is all right for the group to disregard its original plans.

A NOTE ABOUT APATHY

"Apathy" is a word that is heard frequently when people get together to discuss problems. Groups whose members display a lack of enthusiasm or interest must deal with this concern.

Apathetic reactions can occur within a group for different reasons. An individual group member may feel excluded by the rest of the group. All of the members may feel overwhelmed by the big job ahead of them and may give up rather than acknowledge their feelings of helplessness. Sometimes apathy is the result of some external problem and is not connected with the group.

It is helpful for the leadership to take responsibility for dealing with group apathy when it occurs. It is probably best to approach individuals in private about this concern; it may be easier for them to talk honestly under such circumstances, and they may respond to the personal attention and caring that such contact implies. Bringing up the subject of apathy in a group discussion does not work well; people may feel blamed and may not open up when confronted with their own negative behavior and lack of responsiveness.

The onset of apathy may be prevented by stressing positive happenings within the group's life. Group members should acknowledge and congratulate each other when things go well. Individuals should know that their contributions, no matter how small, are important and appreciated. When group successes are celebrated on a regular basis, the members' awareness of their effectiveness is increased.

In most cases the leadership needs to take initial responsibility for recognizing success points during a group's history. Other group members then observe this recognition process and eventually begin to give each other positive reinforcement more spontaneously. When this reinforcement takes place on a regular basis, the members develop themselves into a strong, high-energy group.

Recognizing and acknowledging personal successes of individual group members is part of the larger group self-evaluation process. A group is effective in managing change when its short-term objectives contribute toward achieving its long-range goals—and when the people responsible for those accomplishments are recognized and thanked.

> At one group's annual meeting, awards are given to group members who have made significant contributions of time, energy, or expertise to the group. An article describing the event and mentioning the recipients of awards by name is printed in the neighborhood newspaper, and a photograph of each recipient is included. Most recipients request extra copies of the paper so that they can send the article to friends and relatives.

An end-of-the-year celebration enables a group to formally recognize the efforts of its members, but such recognition should not wait for the end of the year. People need to feel needed. They need to

have a sense of their own value within a group, and they need to feel that they have contributed toward accomplishing group goals. Helping members to identify and meet their personal self-interest needs within a group is essential in order to avoid indifference, and regular support and encouragement from the leadership can make the difference between apathy and enthusiasm.

Action planning can take many forms; it is easy to determine how well a group's planning process works by noticing the levels of energy and involvement among its members. Setting goals and celebrating achievements enable a group's members to learn useful skills while improving their group and reaping personal satisfaction.

RELATED READINGS

Argyris, C. *Intervention theory and method.* Reading, MA: Addison-Wesley, 1970.

Bennis, W. *Changing organizations.* New York: McGraw-Hill, 1966.

Hornstein, H.A., Benedict, B., Burke, W.W., Lewicki, R.J., & Hornstein, M. *Strategies for social change.* New York: Macmillan, 1970.

CHAPTER 7

TOOLS FOR A SUCCESSFUL MEETING

Much of a group's activity takes place in meetings, some of which are productive and some of which seem to be a waste of time. The fact that some meetings are successful and some are not might be accidental, but there are techniques to ensure success and to minimize the chance of wasting time.

When people are asked what characterizes a successful meeting, they respond in a variety of ways. The following is a sampling of these responses:

- People leave feeling satisfied.
- People leave looking forward to the next meeting.
- Everyone agrees that something was accomplished.
- Everyone involved attends and arrives on time.
- People stay until the meeting ends.
- Decisions are clear.
- There is discussion of both facts and feelings about issues.
- People have an opportunity to use their skills and to develop new ones.
- Conflicts are dealt with rather than avoided.
- Rewards are given for individual accomplishments.

Other criteria may be added to this list. The point is that success can be defined by the group itself.

DECIDING HOW TO MAKE DECISIONS

One of the keys to success in meetings is to regularly discuss the group's decision-making processes. As emphasized in Chapter 5, no decision-making approach is inherently better than another; a group's members must decide which approach works best for that group. Many groups decide that following *Robert's Rules of Order* is the best way to run their meetings. Other groups prefer informal discussion and decisions by consensus. No group should automatically slide into a particular mode of operating; instead, the members of the group should discuss various ways to run their meetings.

Some groups protest when the idea of "deciding how to decide" comes up. Either they are not quite sure how to handle such a discussion, or they do not want to take time away from what they consider to be more important agenda items. However, discussing processes is essential; avoiding such discussions can result in ineffective group activity.

The choice regarding the best process to use in certain circumstances depends on several factors: the subject matter, the dynamics of the issue under discussion, and the preferences of the group members. If the leader asks the members which style they prefer, they can arrive at their own best answer.

Occasionally a group decides not to make a decision, and the issue is settled by default.

> A community-planning group was considering whether or not to accept business people who were not residents of the community as voting members. There were two distinct factions within the group, both equally vociferous and both equally sure of their own positions. The group decided not to act; any motions that came up were defeated, and the item was eventually tabled indefinitely.

The inaction of the group in this situation left the status quo intact; no new voting members were admitted to the group.

It is also obvious that a group does not want to make a decision when its members physically or mentally "tune out." This development can be observed by watching the body language of the members; they may start whispering, get up and leave, or postpone an issue on the pretext that there is not enough information available.

Thus, the decision not to decide can be made either actively or passively. The important consideration is to make the decision not to decide a conscious one; otherwise, the group is left with no closure of the issue at hand.

A FEW WORDS ABOUT ROLES

The task and maintenance roles within a group need not be static. The summarizer role, for instance, may be rotated among four different people in attendance at one meeting. In contrast, responsibility for keeping a group focused on its agenda may be delegated to a different person at each meeting.

Most groups have someone to chair the meeting (called the *president, convener, or chairperson*), someone to take minutes (called the *secretary, recording scribe, or recorder*), and someone to oversee money matters (called the *treasurer or financial officer*). The job descriptions for each position vary considerably, and it is important for the group to reach agreement regarding what is expected from each officer. It is best to agree about the responsibilities for each position before the positions are filled.

An unwritten rule is that the presiding officer acts primarily as a moderator, rather than a lobbyist, to encourage people to speak out, to present issues, and to facilitate full discussion.

One group member can be designated the *communicator*, whose function is to keep in touch with the members and to relay their concerns, questions, or issues to the total group. The communicator listens to the pulse of the group as a whole, diagnosing trouble spots early and seeking remedies before a major crisis develops. It is important that the communicator be cautious about exerting undue influence on group members. The communicator's role is to relay information rather than to interpret or advocate on the basis of that information.

As discussed previously, another role is that of the *fair witness* or *process observer*, who, with the explicit sanction of the group, observes how the group is working and tells the group what he or she sees.

The other roles can be shared and rotated freely within the group (see Chapter 5). Specific roles can be delegated if the group feels a special need, or individual members can choose different roles for their own growth. The various roles can help the group function more effectively. A facilitator can identify specific roles and can invite a group to use them when that group is having trouble.

BASIC COMMUNICATION SKILLS

Human-relations specialists, psychologists, consultants, trainers, and others have paid considerable attention to the importance of developing good "communication skills." When people have trouble communicating, the basic problem is that the message *intended* is different from the message *received*. The result can be a misunderstanding or a breakdown in communications between the two affected parties. This principle applies to all forms of communication: *verbal* (words), *nonverbal* (body language and gestures), and *symbolic* (the ways in which individuals dress or wear their hair).

The following diagram [10] represents a summary of what happens when two people, A and B, try to communicate:

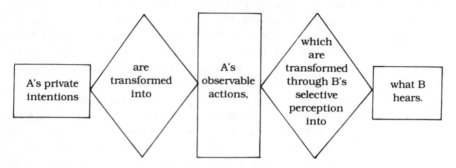

Satir, a well-known figure in the human-potential movement, has developed a simple way to envision communication patterns. This system is described as follows: [11]

An individual can view any situation in which he or she and at least one other person are interacting as having three important components: *me, you* (one or many), and the *context* (the issue and/or substance of the interaction). Effective communication takes all three into account. Statements that suggest that *I* count, *you* count, and the *situation* counts facilitate congruent communicating.

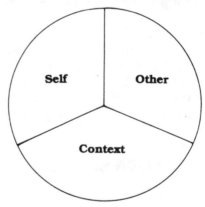

---

[10]Adapted from "The Interpersonal Gap," written by John Wallen, Northwest Regional Educational Laboratory, Portland, Oregon. Published in *Interpersonal Communications* by Xicom, Inc., 1972. In the public domain.

[11] Adapted from Satir, V. PEOPLEMAKING, pp. 59-80. Palo Alto, California: Science and Behavior Books, 1972. Used with permission.

[12]From Satir, V., *Making Contact*, Celestial Arts, 1976. Used with permission.

When one of the three elements is not considered, the communication is garbled and dysfunctional. For example, the responses to a situation in which two people are dealing with a broken flower vase might represent any one of the following styles.

The *blamer* operates in a manner that says "I count; you don't count." The blamer might respond to the situation by pointing a finger at another person and saying "It's your fault that the vase broke" or "If it weren't for you, everything would be fine." It makes no difference who actually broke the vase. The blamer's style is to look for someone to blame, regardless of the facts in the matter.

The *placater* uses a style that discounts the self and implies "I don't count; you count." The placater might assume a woeful expression and use words such as "I'll never do that again" or "I always mess things up." Again, the facts are not really important to the placater, whose style is to avoid conflict by taking responsibility for the problem.

The *computer* disregards both self and others by saying "The people aren't the issue; the situation is the issue." The computer might respond to the flower-vase situation with the comment "Let's not get excited. Let's sit down and calmly figure out what can be done."

The *distracter* ignores all three components of effective communication and operates in a manner that says "I don't count, you don't count, and the situation doesn't count." The distracter might make a joke about the situation and suggest that the parties involved go out for an ice-cream sundae.

Some people use dysfunctional communication styles with particular relationships or groups. To evaluate the effectiveness of your own communication style, try the following: Tape a meeting or a conversation that you are a part of and then listen to the tape with a friend. Determine which of your statements represent the styles just described. Then consider what changes, if any, you want to make.

There are preventive measures to protect against communication breakdowns. These basic techniques have been developed by various members of the human-potential movement, beginning with the National Training Lab in the late Forties.

Wallen developed the following categories, which outline the four basic skills for improving interpersonal communications:[13]

1. *Paraphrasing* (showing concern with ideas and suggestions). This skill consists of letting the other person know what meaning has been attributed to his or her statements. It is used for the purpose of acknowledging and checking for accuracy in understanding.

- "Do you mean [Statement]?"
- "Is this an accurate understanding of your idea? [Statement]"
- "Would this be an example of what you mean? [Specific example]"

2. *Checking perceptions* (showing concern for the other person and his or her feelings). This skill involves describing one's perceptions of the other person's feelings and doing so tentatively and without evaluating him or her.

- "I get the impression that you'd rather not talk about this. Is that the case?"
- "Were you disappointed that they didn't ask you?"
- "You look as if you feel hurt by my comment. Do you?"

3. *Describing behavior.* When using this skill, one describes specific, observable actions of the other person; inferences, accusations, or generalizations about that person's motives, attitudes, or personality traits are not stated.

- "You bumped my cup" rather than "You never watch where you're going."

---

[13]Adapted from "Summary of Basic Communications Skills for Improving Interpersonal Relationships," written by John Wallen, Northwest Regional Educational Laboratory, Portland, Oregon. Published in *Interpersonal Communications* by Xicom, Inc., 1972. In the public domain.

- "Jim and Bill have done most of the talking, and the rest of us have said very little" rather than "Jim and Bill always have to be in the spotlight."

4. *Describing feelings.* This skill consists of identifying one's feelings by name or simile as well as action urge. This identification is conveyed as information about one's inner state and not as an accusation or a coercive demand.

- "I felt hurt when you ignored my comment" rather than "You're rude!"
- "I feel hurt and embarrassed" rather than "You just put me down!"
- "I'm disappointed that you forgot" rather than "You don't care about me."
- "I'm too angry to listen to any more now" rather than "Get away from me!"

The net effect of using the basic communication skills is to open up lines of communication, ensuring understanding and validating the remarks made by the other person. The suggested responses invite clarification and a cooperative relationship between the involved parties.

PREPARING FOR MEETINGS

If group members are expected to come to a meeting, they must be informed of the time and place—in advance. The selected meeting time should be one that is convenient for the membership, and the selected location should be accessible. Regularly scheduled meeting dates are often a good idea so that people can plan ahead and set aside that particular time each week or month. If meeting notices are written, some idea of what is going to be discussed should be included. A sample meeting notice is provided in Figure 3.

The physical arrangement of the meeting room can play a part in whether the group members feel comfortable. If possible, chairs and tables should be arranged so that everyone can see each other. A U-shape or a rectangular arrangement can be effective. If there are no tables, chairs should be arranged in a circle, rather than in rows, to let the members know that each counts as much as the others. Someone should check out the meeting room ahead of time so that any missing supplies can be obtained; in addition, someone should find out where extra chairs can be located if needed and whether coffee or tea will be available.

When a particularly friendly or social atmosphere is desired, it is a good idea to meet at someone's home so that people can feel freer to express their ideas. However, although a formal meeting room can be intimidating, it may be appropriate if the subject matter is formal. Various room arrangements can be experimented with as a way of injecting some variety into the meeting format; then the members can decide which they like best.

SETTING AN AGENDA

It is important that group members have an opportunity to be involved with developing the agenda. This involvement gives them a stake in carrying out the agenda and opens up the process of deciding what the group priorities will be. After the agenda has been

You are invited to the February meeting of . . .

CENTRAL COMMUNITY COUNCIL

Tuesday, February 8th

7:30 p.m.

1900 11th Avenue South

(Emmanuel Methodist Church;

enter on 19th Street side)

Items to be discussed include:

- City Council motion to decrease housing money for our community: Do we want to take some action?

- Publicity planning for upcoming neighborhood elections: Who is going to do what, and when?

- Reports from neighborhood representatives: What is happening in our community?

- Other items that people at the meeting want to discuss or announce.

Participation in this meeting is open to all! If you need transportation or have questions, call Eileen at 874-5369.

Figure 3. Sample Meeting Notice

---

developed, the group members should be invited to make additions and deletions if they feel any are needed. Figure 4 provides a sample agenda format that others have found useful; it sets the tone for group involvement and gives the members an idea of what to expect.

The proposed agenda can be put together in advance by a few group members, or it can be drawn up at the meeting. Generally, some advance planning is better so that any necessary preparation, such as duplication of handouts, can be done. Members are more likely to come if they have an idea of what will be discussed; providing them with this information also gives them a chance to prepare individually if they wish to do so.

The key components of the sample agenda format are the term "proposed" (or "suggested") agenda, the review of the agenda itself as an explicit item, and the provision for "other" items to be added. Posting the agenda on a wall can help focus the members' attention

PROPOSED AGENDA
October 12th

(1 minute)	1. Call to order.
(5 minutes)	2. Review and approval of agenda.
(5 minutes)	3. Review and approval of minutes.
(10 minutes)	4. Announcements:
	• Upcoming contracts
	• Production
	• Other
(30 minutes)	5. Presentation by Product-Development Task Force: decision on continuing development of the new product line.
(20 minutes)	6. Annual meeting: Finalize organizational plans.
(? minutes)	7. Other: _____
(5 minutes)	8. Critique of the meeting: "I liked," "I disliked," "I learned" statements from group.
	9. Adjournment.

Figure 4. Sample Agenda Format

---

at the start, and they can see the items checked off as they are covered.

The time limits next to the agenda items can be considered as guidelines. If the group is involved in an intense debate, the chairperson should use discretion about whether or not to cut off the discussion. Sometimes it is sufficient to comment that the time has run out; then someone can suggest an extension, or the discussion can be summarized.

Making announcements can be a casual way to start the meeting. New members can be introduced, visitors can be welcomed, and the tone of the meeting can be established. Groups vary in the degree of comfort they feel with a casual beginning; some like this style while others prefer dealing with informalities after the meeting. If the chairperson is not sure which style is preferred, a discussion of this subject should be included as an agenda item.

BRINGING IN NEW MEMBERS

The first meeting attended by new members often sets their impressions. If someone new feels welcome and a part of the group from the start, he or she is more likely to become an active participant. If possible, a premeeting orientation should be conducted by a member who is familiar with the group's work. Also, a formal orientation packet can be prepared to hand out to new people. Another valuable approach is to assign a partner to each new member; this individual sits next to the new person and explains what happens during the meeting. The partner may also check with the new member after the meeting to answer any questions and to offer informal orientation.

The initial contact with a new member is a good time to share any group norms. If the group prefers to make decisions by consensus, it is helpful to inform a new person of this preference. If the group has stated that all opinions are important, the new person should be encouraged to ask questions and to share ideas. All of the group's previously adopted "rules" should be communicated to new people so that they know their status. Pertinent written material, especially statements of purpose or bylaws and incorporation documents, should be given to new members as soon as possible. Past minutes and other records can also be made available.

KEEPING PEOPLE INTERESTED

Nothing is more frustrating than to be a member of a group and to be confused about that group's activities. Many of such a person's questions are never asked because he or she is afraid that these questions will waste the other members' time. Eventually the person experiencing this problem loses interest in the group.

The chairperson can play an active part in maintaining a group's interest level by offering opportunities for people to ask questions, by expressing a need for clarification, and by making sure that the members share a common knowledge base for making decisions. A brief review of a discussion, for instance, can remind people of the group's progress on various tasks, bring new members up to date, point out misunderstandings, and focus the conversation in a useful direction. It is also a good idea for someone other than the chairperson to provide the review so that as much participation as possible is generated. Asking open-ended questions that permit sharing of opinions lets people know that their ideas are welcome; "yes" or "no" questions discourage participation.

If the discussion lags or if the members' energy level seems especially low, this development should be brought to the attention of the full group. Sometimes, however, if the hour is late and people are tired, it is not wise to press the matter. On other occasions people lose interest because they are afraid to express their true feelings. Offering an opportunity to talk about the group atmosphere is often useful in re-establishing enthusiasm.

HELPING GROUP MEMBERS SHARE THEIR OPINIONS

Group members too frequently leave a meeting feeling frustrated and angry because they did not express their opinions or because someone monopolized the discussion. This situation does not have to arise; certain techniques can be used to foster more open discussion and to deal with monopolizers quickly. Often the leader is aware ahead of time that particular issues will be controversial. In this case he or she can spend some time prior to the meeting reviewing possible ways to facilitate discussion of these issues.

Process suggestions that can be proposed to a group include the following:

- Allowing time for each individual in the room (guests included) to express a personal view. Everyone is given a time limit as well as the right to "pass" without making a statement.
- Asking the group members to think through their opinions and then to take turns voicing them on an equal-time basis.
- Recording opinions on a chalkboard or newsprint as they are stated, reminding people not to repeat an idea after it has been recorded.
- Asking the members to take turns completing a sentence such as "I would vote no (or yes) on this proposal because . . . ." A time limit is suggested for each completion.
- Requesting that the group list the positive and negative viewpoints of the issue, with the object of presenting as much information as possible.

Groups often have trouble expressing opposition to an idea that is on the floor. Some helpful statements to invite criticism and objections are as follows:

- "Does anyone have a problem with that idea?"
- "Does anyone feel especially uncomfortable about that?"
- "Let's take some time to see if there are negative implications involved with the direction we're pursuing."

- "Let's alternate 'pro' and 'con' viewpoints in response to this motion."

The premise behind taking this action is that unless people have a chance to express objections during the decision-making process, the resulting decisions will not be as sound. If someone feels that he or she has been excluded from the discussion, resentments may arise later and the final decision may be sabotaged in some way.

ENCOURAGING GROUP SELF-AWARENESS

The process politician, whether in the role of chairperson, group member, or outside observer, can call a group's attention to its collaboration processes. If there seems to be tension during a meeting, for instance, the process politician might say, "I'm feeling tension in the room right now, and it's getting in my way. Is anyone else aware of that feeling?" This type of simple, "I" statement can help a group deal with its maintenance problems at the moment of their occurrence. By demonstrating such interventions, the process politician is assuming the role of "educator" and is actually teaching group-process skills.

Another way in which a group can develop self-awareness is to periodically evaluate the members' ability to work together. This may be done by canvassing all members to find out how they felt about the last meeting, or it may be done through the use of maintenance checks during a regular group session (see Chapter 5 and the Appendix).

Group members can also increase their awareness of the various aspects of group behavior by completing process-observation report forms (see Chapter 5). An individual member can voluntarily begin using the process-observation report form, or all members can participate in rating their interactions.

End-of-meeting critique sessions are also useful self-awareness devices. During such sessions the group members reveal what they liked about the meeting, what could have been better, and how they are feeling at the moment. These critiques provide guidelines for improving future meetings. This same type of checkup can be written into an evaluation form that members complete before leaving the meeting. The important thing is to use this information to help members feel better about their participation and the work of the group.

HELPING MEMBERS TO "RETIRE"

No one can be expected to be a group member forever. Members leave a group for a variety of reasons as their needs and the group's focus change. A letter of resignation should be responded to personally, preferably by the group's chairperson, so that there is an opportunity to find out privately whether the member is leaving for personal reasons or because of some dissatisfaction with the way in which the group is functioning.

"Retiring" members should be encouraged to personally inform the group of their leaving. This practice provides an opportunity for discussion of transition procedures, if needed, and allows the group to achieve closure of its relationship with the member who is leaving.

Such an occasion is also a good time to take advantage of the retiring member's expertise by asking for his or her suggestions for future issues that the group might consider. In some cases the retiring member might be asked to suggest someone who could be invited to join, so that there are no gaps in the membership.

TERMINATING A GROUP

Sometimes the best thing that can happen to a group is its dissolution. For this reason it is important that a group establish measurable, specific tasks to be accomplished; once the job has been completed the group can disband.

In addition, it is often proper for a group to take a recess from time to time. If there has been consistently low participation and the members have exhibited low energy levels, this development could be an indication that the members have other, more important priorities at the time (such as the winter holidays). Rather than rival such priorities, it is wise to acknowledge the group members' feelings and to make alternate plans. For example, canceling a meeting and having a social event instead might provide the change of pace that is needed.

If a group's job has ended officially or if the group's term of office has expired, it is a good idea to deal directly with the group members' feelings about such a situation. A celebration of some kind, during which the members formally recognize the termination of their group, is important in achieving a sense of completion. The members might want to exchange addresses, arrange to get together again in the near future, or just say "good-bye" in a way that is comfortable.

Making a conscious decision that a group should be dissolved is difficult, but sometimes this is the best alternative. If this decision is the right one, after disbanding the members will feel relieved and free to pursue other interests.

> Whether a group chooses to operate with a highly structured or a more flexible style, it is important that its members be familiar with some of the techniques that can be used to ensure successful meetings. This knowledge is applicable in any group setting, can enhance group life, and encourages broad participation.

RELATED READINGS

Bradford, L.P. *Making meetings work: A guide for leaders and group members.* San Diego, CA: University Associates, 1976.

Satir, V. *Peoplemaking.* Palo Alto, CA: Science & Behavior Books, 1972.

Schindler-Rainman, E., & Lippitt, R. *Taking your meetings out of the doldrums.* San Diego, CA: University Associates, 1975.

CHAPTER 8

BEHIND-THE-SCENES ACTIVITY

A group's activities continue even when its members are not meeting. Much of what enters into group decision making happens outside the meeting format.

The term "extragroup dynamics" describes those activities that are relevant to a group's growth and progress and that take place outside the formal meetings. Good process politicians acknowledge the importance of these dynamics; they recognize that any outside interaction, whether task or process oriented, is part of a group's development. Informal contacts between group members are, in many cases, more economical in terms of time, energy, and so forth than are formal meetings.

Groups that deal with complex systems and institutional structures need behind-the-scenes contacts. Not everything can be done within the confines of a meeting. A group's members need time to get to know each other. They need a chance to think through their personal and group goals, and they need to do the background work or information seeking that precedes decision making. To determine your own experience with behind-the-scenes group activity, try the following: Think about a group of which you are an active member. List the kinds of behind-the-scenes contacts that you have had with other members. For each of these contacts, who initiated the encounter, what was the content, and what was the result? How many of the contacts were instances in which people were asking for advice? How many were simply occasions for sharing personal frustrations or feelings about the events of the last meeting? How many were oriented toward planning for the future? How many of the contacts had a bearing, either positive or negative, on the way in which the members work together?

It is important to be aware of what happens between meetings and to know how to use such situations productively.

EXTRAGROUP DYNAMICS

The phases of group development—dependence, counterdependence, and interdependence—were discussed in Chapter 5. This kind of development takes place outside the meeting room as well as during formal meetings. In fact, at least 75 percent of the work in which groups are involved can take place outside the formal decision-making process. Within almost any group, decisions are often made well in advance of the final vote, regardless of whether the members have consciously chosen to operate in that manner. Anyone who wants to be influential in a group or community needs to remember that much of the action takes place behind the scenes.

Behind-the-scenes action is not bad; it is simply a fact of life. Without it, many meetings would be a waste of time.

Some activities that typically happen between meetings are as follows:

- The chairperson contacts members for ideas about the agenda for the next meeting.
- A new member requests an information session with a committee person.
- Two members arrange to have lunch together.

- One member researches other groups that are working on issues that her group is concerned about.
- The secretary types and distributes or mails the minutes.

The concept of extragroup dynamics emphasizes that a group does not stop developing after a meeting is adjourned. Struggles and growing pains are dealt with behind the scenes, and the group starts its subsequent meeting with additional activity that rarely shows up in the minutes.

A meeting of a board of directors was held with the head table looking out over rows of folding chairs. Three days after the meeting, the chairperson received a phone call from a relatively new member who wanted to know why such a formal seating arrangement had been used. The new member recommended that a less formal style be used, with chairs in a casual circle and all members facing one another. For the next meeting, chairs were arranged in a circle. The new member resolved her personal concern about the group by initiating this change and thus became a contributing member of the total board.

As a rule it is useful for a group member to plan to spend as much time on group work outside meetings as he or she does in the meeting room. Meetings held prior to a total-group meeting, for instance, often help members to prepare for an issue so that in the total-group meeting the discussion flows smoothly and all aspects of the issue are considered. This does not mean that solutions should be offered to the group as finished proposals; such a practice would be contrary to the philosophy of process politics. The purpose of planning is to determine how to handle a specific issue, to think about long-range goals, and to consider ways to accomplish these goals.

The members of the planning committee decided to spend their next meeting discussing subsidized housing. Because this was seen as a broad topic, the committee officers spent several hours before the meeting contacting members to find out what was of interest to them. They gathered resources and invited technical experts to the meeting. They also put together a suggested agenda for the meeting. No specific expectations were established ahead of time; these activities were carried out to plan the process for facilitating discussion during the total-committee meeting.

In many ways the process politician is most active in the extragroup arena.

In one particular group it was the process politician who first called attention to the fact that a number of group members were frustrated with the way in which meetings were being conducted. John, the chairperson, had no idea that the members experienced his style as threatening. The process politician suggested that John elicit feedback from the members over the telephone. John followed this suggestion, and group satisfaction and productivity were heightened after a group discussion concerning the best procedure for making decisions.

A process politician can help a group's leadership keep in touch with the pulse of the group. The process politician has a responsibility to bring group concerns to the attention of the leaders and to suggest ways to deal with those concerns, in much the same way that an ombudsperson seeks to facilitate healthy group functioning.

SPECIFIC ACTIVITIES

A variety of activities can take place between formal meetings. These activities can include task, maintenance, or logistical functions. Some require extensive time, and others can be conducted during telephone encounters. Some of the task-oriented activities include the following:

- Establishing individual members' responsibilities;
- Posting announcements on bulletin boards;
- Developing a strategy for dealing with the latest management directives;
- Doing research on a new product design;
- Reaching out to potential new members;
- Checking with group members regarding their ideas for the next meeting's agenda;
- Investigating rumors;
- Seeking advice from experts;
- Lobbying for issues that the group supports; and
- Following through on assignments delegated at the last meeting.

All of these activities deal with accomplishing tasks that are relevant to the goals of a group. Another type of behind-the-scenes activity has to do with group membership and the interactions that can pull members together or alienate them. Although these types of activities may not have a direct bearing on the accomplishment of group goals, they do affect the attitudes and commitment of the members, who ultimately are responsible for making or breaking a group. Such activities include the following:

- Checking with new members to determine their expectations;
- Socializing with a potential group member to establish personal rapport;
- Unwinding after a meeting with other group members;
- Reflecting privately about the group events of the previous months;
- Establishing friendships with other members who previously have been only acquaintances;
- Asking for advice on ways in which to handle a disruptive group participant;
- Straightening out personal conflicts between group members, possibly with the help of a third party; and
- Forming coalitions both within and outside the group.

In addition, many behind-the-scenes activities, such as the following, must be consciously planned and arranged in advance.

- Distributing meeting announcements;
- Cleaning up after a meeting;
- Maintaining attendance records and reviewing them to ensure that memberships do not lapse;
- Keeping financial records up to date;
- Preparing refreshments to be served at meetings; and
- Arranging transportation for members as necessary.

The handling of the basic mechanics sets a tone that either encourages or discourages member involvement. A group that is extremely disorganized may not be able to cope with more complicated issues.

It is important to remember that all of these different types of activities are part of a group's development and history and that it is both appropriate and helpful for most of them to happen in extragroup settings. If these matters were not taken care of in this way, little would be accomplished during formal group sessions.

BEHIND-THE-SCENES PERSONALITIES

To begin thinking about behind-the-scenes personalities, try the following: First think of a group to which you belong. Then consider the people with whom you come in contact as you deal with your group and its projects. Are they all group members? Are they all volunteers? What functions do they serve during your contacts with them?

Many of the people who are important to a group's development never attend a meeting but provide valuable assistance nonetheless. It is helpful to reconsider the roles that were identified in Chapter 5 as necessary for effective group functioning. Basically, behind-the-scenes personalities fall into the same role categories, but their activities take place outside the group.

Bob, who had been hired by the city to provide staff support to a community group, usually served as an information provider. He also functioned as a third-party sounding board for the group's chairperson between meetings. Bob did not consider himself to be a bona-fide group member, but his behind-the-scenes involvement with group members definitely helped to shape the group's growth.

Process politicians often assume certain support roles to groups, and in this capacity they try to maintain their separateness from the groups with which they work. However, the idea that such people are truly separate from group functioning is subject to question. Even though a process politician may not be a voting group member, that person can serve to promote and enrich group effectiveness. This concept ties in primarily with maintenance functions, for which the process politician's efforts focus on communicating members' concerns to the group.

One part of Bob's function in providing staff support for the community group was to observe the process during meetings and to share his feedback with group members between meetings. He offered his comments as food for thought, listened to the reactions, and later formulated suggestions about ways to help make things go more smoothly. These suggestions were discussed with group members informally; subsequently, if there was group support, the suggestions were brought before the entire group for consideration.

In this situation the staff member was in the role of *fair witness* or *process observer*, as discussed in Chapter 2, even though the fair-witness feedback took place behind the scenes.

A variety of consultants contribute to group success and progress without ever attending a meeting. It is important to make use of the idea that everyone is a consultant because people like to be asked for their opinions.

The members of the neighborhood-improvement group realized that they needed some fund-raising assistance. They decided to make use of their personal contacts in various fields. Each group member agreed to approach a potential "consultant" to solicit his or her professional advice about fund-raising techniques. No one who was approached refused to help; in fact, all of those contacted felt flattered to be seen as people with knowledge that could be useful to others.

Every community or group has access to unlimited resources. No organization needs to feel limited by its membership list or its budget. It is a valuable practice to call on behind-the-scenes resource people.

Some groups formalize the functions of a resource consultant by hiring someone to provide time-limited expertise on a particular subject. The creative use of consultants between meetings can both enrich a group and build contacts outside that group.

The leadership of a group or committee cannot take total responsibility for the functions that take place behind the scenes. What is important is to acknowledge that it is natural for people to talk about issues among themselves; it is also important to see that discussion process as a valuable opportunity for people to learn about each other and about changing issues.

CHAPTER 9

THE ROLE OF CONFLICT: USING TENSION CREATIVELY

The following is an example of one group's reaction to the subject of conflict.

An agency staff decided to have an in-service training workshop on conflict. The group members arrived knowing only that the subject for the evening was how to deal effectively with conflict. There was obvious tension in the air; the members sat silently, looked around nervously, and waited for the meeting to begin. The training staff joined the group and began the session by inviting the group members to share the feelings they had experienced while waiting. As the members responded, reasons for their anxiety came out: "I was afraid someone would become angry." "I didn't want to cry in front of the group." "Conflict is such a negative thing that I was afraid we might tear down some of the good things about this group."

The responses of the group members were predictable. People are anxious about conflict and even about discussions of conflict. This anxiety may be a result of fear that the conflict will destroy the group, or it may come from a desire to avoid angry feelings.

It is unfortunate that conflict has only negative connotations. In reality it is a natural result of diversity because the members of any group have different values, self-interests, and points of view. Healthy groups encourage their members to contribute and to ask for what they want. Whether in a group or a relationship, conflict is a natural condition of being alive. A group that does not experience conflict is probably not very creative, active, or strong. On the other hand, unresolved conflict can tear a group apart.

Groups experience conflicts of various types:

- Disagreements over the problems that the group should be working on;

- Differences of opinion regarding the way in which to accomplish the group's goals;
- Feelings of rejection on the part of one or several members; and
- Confusion about whose opinions are most valued.

The role of the process politician is to help a group acknowledge and deal with conflicts as they arise—to *manage conflict.* Unless conflict is managed in some way, it produces random or haphazard changes.

With effective management, conflict situations can advance a group's interest and health. A group that successfully tackles a tough situation emerges healthier and stronger than one that fails to recognize and work on conflict issues.

CONFLICT AS THE CONTEXT FOR CHANGE

Change and conflict go hand in hand. There is a direct correlation between the rate of change experienced by a group and the amount of conflict that is present within that group: the faster the change, the greater the degree of conflict. The process politician helps to manage change and conflict so that a group moves toward its goals rather than away from them.

The natural tendency for a group is to resist rapid change, although even the status-quo situation is not always perfectly static. The status quo is maintained by the desire of members not to alter the group's traditions or the members' self-interests. Some forces drive toward the group's goals; others restrain progress toward goals (Lewin, 1969). When these two sets of forces are in balance, the status quo is maintained.

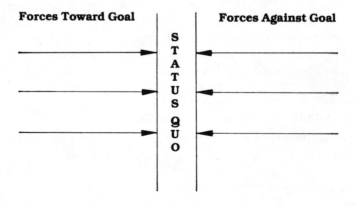

When the two sets of forces are thrown out of balance, conflict occurs. A new force comes into play, or an old force is no longer present. The status quo is jarred, and the group begins to question its position, its future, and its very existence. By the time the forces are in balance again, there could be a new status quo that is either favorable (closer to the goal) or unfavorable (farther from the goal). Thus, in essence, conflict changes a situation; the status quo continues it.

MAKING CONFLICT WORK POSITIVELY

The key to making a conflict situation work positively is to think that it can. The members of a group that is experiencing conflict should remind each other of the exciting possibilities; in this way the tension created by such a situation often generates new ideas. Considering conflict to be creative tension can help to break through old ways of thinking.

It is not necessary for the process politician to create artificial conflicts in a group. What the process politician needs to do is to help group members to recognize conflict and to acknowledge it to themselves and each other. After acknowledging the presence of conflict, it is important to understand that for a while the group members will experience it as a problem. They need time for this. However, it is not a good idea to stay focused on conflict as a problem any longer than necessary. An experienced process politician knows when a group is ready to start working on solutions and takes action to bring about the working process.

At times when the status quo has been disturbed, process politicians as change agents need to consolidate their energy in a way that achieves a new status quo. If the process politician perceives that he or she is causing the conflict or that other group members are responsible, it may be necessary to call on an uninvolved third party to help.

It is important for a group's members to be aware of the ways in which they respond to conflict. In general terms, people show either a flight or a fight response. If they possess basic skills for managing conflict, they are less likely to avoid and more willing to resolve the issue at hand.

CONFLICT-RESOLUTION SKILLS

Conflict resolution occurs when the parties to the conflict understand each other's stance accurately and proceed on the basis of those agreements or disagreements. Clear communicating is the basis for managing conflicts. Too often individuals who are arguing misinterpret each other and come to conclusions that seriously miss the mark. It is helpful to review the communication skills outlined in Chapter 7 and to keep in mind that miscommunication is the source of many conflicts.

The process politician can help people to use their power effectively by encouraging them to seek out their personal support-group members to ventilate and clarify feelings about a conflict situation. He or she can also help people in conflict to think in creative ways. An approach that is very useful is called the "win/win" style, which can be illustrated as follows:

$$
\begin{aligned}
\text{You lose/I lose} &= \text{Lose/lose} \\
\text{You win/I lose} &= \text{Win/lose} \\
\text{You lose/I win} &= \text{Lose/win} \\
\text{You win/I win} &= \text{Win/win}
\end{aligned}
$$

Approaching conflicts from the standpoint of looking for *win/win* results encourages people to work together for mutually beneficial solutions. The win/win approach takes into account the self-interest issues at stake and maximizes chances for everyone involved. to obtain at least part of what he or she wants. Win/win emphasizes shared problem solving rather than conflict resolution through competition.

STEPS FOR CONFLICT RESOLUTION

The following are the basic steps for conflict resolution:

1. *Recognize that a conflict exists.* Conflict, in and of itself, is neither good nor bad. It has no inherent moral quality, and its impact depends largely on the way in which people respond to it. Although conflict is neutral, people do not respond to it neutrally. They run from it, prepare to fight, or pretend that it does not exist. Facing conflict can increase the effectiveness of a group or a relationship, and it can build intimacy and understanding.

Eileen belonged to one particular group for several years. She felt frustrated about the group's activities, so she shared her frustrations with the group. The resulting eruption forced new group dynamics and broke a stalemate that had been uncomfortable for everyone.

Admitting to oneself that there might be a problem is the first step toward conflict management. A problem can be ignored, but ignoring it does not make it go away; sooner or later it manifests itself, perhaps disguised as something else. Avoidance behavior also can divert energy from a group's goal.

2. *Acknowledge to the group that there is a conflict.* Before a group can begin to resolve a conflict, its members must acknowledge aloud that a problem exists. No matter how it is brought up, the mention of conflict issues helps to surface other feelings that group members have been keeping to themselves. Turmoil occurs, and the members find it difficult to see beyond the hassles raised by the conflict. They may become "stuck" at this stage unless something is done fairly quickly.

Members need encouragement to express their feelings freely in response to the identification of a conflict issue. Voicing emotional reactions at this point is important in and of itself. Unless there is a chance to vent anger or resentment, the group will not be able to approach the conflict from a rational point of view, and resolution will be difficult.

3. *Diagnose the conflict.* The third step is to develop an understanding of the nature of the conflict. It is difficult, especially when strong emotions are aroused, for a group to move into the diagnosis phase of conflict management. For this reason it is essential for the process politician to take action immediately. He or she can contact individual group members behind the scenes to provide a listening ear and also to begin exploring what is causing their emotional responses. It is also important that the process politician help the members see the possibilities for resolution if everyone agrees to work toward it.

Diagnosing conflict involves finding out as much as possible about what is happening, who is involved, and whose feelings are the strongest. The struggle may be mainly one individual's personal struggle that other group members do not understand, or it may be a situation in which two group members are vying for power. Conflict can exist between two people or between groups within the same system.

Knowing the main characters helps in understanding a conflict. People with personal stakes in a conflict have difficulty in seeing ways to resolve it. Under these circumstances the process politician can ask the group members who do not have personal stakes to be creative and to think of ways to resolve the conflict successfully.

After the people in conflict have been identified, the next procedure is to find out the type of conflict that is being dealt with. Sometimes the disagreement is over goals.

The members of the travel club decided that they wanted to take a winter trip together. Disagreement arose because some members wanted to ski and some wanted to go to a warm climate. Thus, their goals were in conflict.

Sometimes group members agree on goals but are in conflict over the way to accomplish those goals.

Last year the travel club decided to go to New Orleans together. Three members wanted to drive, while the rest insisted on flying. Thus, the conflict centered around the way to achieve the mutually agreed-on goal.

Conflict results from actual or perceived differences in values, resources, needs, styles, or interests. It is important for the process politician to be aware that such individual differences may lead to distrust among group members.

Diagnosing conflict can take place either during group discussions or outside formal meetings, depending on the issue and the group's ability to discuss it. If the group is unable or unwilling to talk, the process politician can contact individuals to share in their perceptions of the group members' interactions with one another.

A teachers' union was unable to focus on conflict diagnosis because the members felt emotionally overwhelmed by the issue. Eileen talked privately with the members and was able to derive a sense of the individual members' diagnoses. When sharing her observations with the executive committee of the union, she tried not to confuse her own perceptions with those of the group members.

4. *Identify individual needs or wants.* To resolve group conflicts it is important for everyone involved to have a clear idea of what each group member wants. Group members can acquire this knowledge by listing their individual criteria for a satisfactory outcome. Someone may need to offer an explanation to the group or apologize for a past mistake. These need/want statements can then be shared aloud or posted. Extra time should be alloted for clarification of statements.

This step prepares the group members for talking about solutions that can meet the group's needs. By this time the members are looking beyond the conflict issue itself and are thinking about conflict resolution.

5. *Identify mutually exclusive needs or wants.* If three group members want to work on resolving the conflict and two others want to drop the whole discussion, it appears that there is a

deadlock. Sometimes a member may personally prefer to drop the discussion but agrees to pursue it in the interest of the group. Members who clarify the degree of flexibility in their need/want statements open up new possibilities for action. However, if there are areas of complete disagreement, it is important for everyone to be aware of these areas.

The process of looking for areas of disagreement can be very productive. Often individuals recognize their own rigid thinking by becoming aware of a variety of perspectives. Also, the process itself becomes a group effort and can help to rebuild bridges.

6. *Identify areas of agreement.* Looking for areas of agreement regarding needs and wants positively opens up the negotiation process. It may seem that no areas of agreement exist until the group consciously looks for them. There may be resistance if the conflict is a long-standing one that has polarized the group members into distinct camps. After the members have decided that they want to work toward resolution, the process politician can help to disband these camps.

A visual illustration of the group's discussion is as follows:

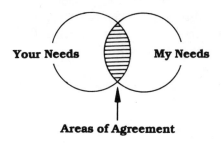

When a group's members concentrate on their areas of agreement, they ensure success for themselves. Also, when people succeed, they find it easier to tackle more difficult problems. The group that pays more attention to the various possibilities wastes less energy on problems.

Sometimes it is impossible to find areas of agreement. A group's members might be able to agree only that they do not want to try to solve a particular problem at a particular time, but even this decision is an agreement. The process politician's role is to help people to be satisfied with the way in which the conflict was approached, even if the outcome is the disbanding of the group.

7. *Develop a plan to act on areas of agreement and follow the plan.* After the areas of agreement have been identified, a group can begin to plan its strategy for action. The result will be an action plan for resolution of the present conflict. The use of action-planning steps (Chapter 6) is appropriate at this point.

The most important points to remember about conflict are as follows:

- The key to making conflict work in a positive way is to remember that conflict, like other problems, is solvable. This assumption tends to bring about solutions.
- Possibilities are more fun than problems—and more effective, too.
- Most situations present more than two possibilities. The group that thinks of a number of possibilities has better chances of finding one that is acceptable.
- Action planning is a way to manage conflict.
- Anyone can learn to be creative and to think of new possibilities. One can train himself or herself to be creative by brainstorming, fantasizing, daydreaming, or meditating.
- Finding overlapping self-interests usually leads to win/win solutions.
- People who take an extremist position can help to surface conflict in a group and to provoke positive (or negative) action.
- The important consideration is not whether conflict exists but how it is dealt with.

REFERENCE

Lewin, K. Quasi-stationary social equilibria and the problem of permanent change. In W.G. Bennis, K.D. Benne, & R. Chin (Eds.), *The planning of change.* New York: Holt, Rinehart and Winston, 1969.

RELATED READINGS

Blake, R.R., Shepard, H.A., & Mouton, J.S. *Managing intergroup conflict in industry.* Houston, TX: Gulf, 1964.

Hall, J. *Conflict management survey.* Conroe, TX: Teleometrics International, 1969.

Walton, R.E. *Interpersonal peacemaking: Confrontations and third party consultation.* Reading, MA: Addison-Wesley, 1969.

CHAPTER 10

HOW TO GET AROUND NOT KNOWING WHAT TO DO

Process politicians frequently find themselves in situations in which they simply do not know what to do next. These are times when all the diagnostic tools and techniques in the world seem irrelevant, and they are unable to come up with appropriate answers. Situations like these are inevitable for those who work with people, and it is important to know ways to handle them. Such occasions present valuable learning opportunities as well.

As discussed previously, problems have multiple solutions. The capacity to figure out these solutions has more to do with one's mind-set than with one's knowledge of techniques. For example, in an emergency people are able to do things they never dreamed they could do; afterward they scarcely believe they actually did those things. This ability to get "unstuck" can be learned and put to work by process politicians.

IDENTIFYING THE SITUATION

Often a process politician thinks that a group is doing well and then suddenly realizes that he or she does not know at all what is happening in the group. In fact, he or she may feel like the cartoon character who has run off the edge of a cliff and does all right until he looks down and realizes that he is standing in midair. Knowing that there will be times when one "runs off the edge" can make it easier to deal with such situations when they happen and can also help to prevent them in the future.

The first step is to learn to recognize the signs that indicate that one might be close to a standstill. One such danger sign is the foxhole syndrome, characterized by pulling back and trying not to be noticed. We all have our "foxholes" or ways of avoiding situations in which we are not comfortable. Because we do not know what to do to change these situations, we retreat and concentrate on pro-

tecting ourselves from unknown consequences. In other words, we are on the defensive.

Sam worked with a business that tried to resolve problems by changing its organizational structure. Departments were reorganized every year. When one of these changes was coming up, the managers' tendency was to hold back and to take no risks in their work until the reorganization had been completed.

Another sign of being "stuck" is the feeling that one's friends or fellow group members are all wrong. It is possible for process politicians to become so involved with their group projects that they do not see the mistakes they are making. They also may have trouble listening to other people who try to point out those mistakes. When a process politician becomes isolated from other group members because of disagreements, this development is a sign of trouble.

"Either/or" thinking is still another indication of being "stuck." The process politician who limits options to only two alternatives can expect problems.

Thus, when a process politician does not know what to do, he or she must first recognize and then admit that this is the case. After this admission has been made, he or she becomes more able to put creativity to work, to ask for help, and to explore new options. There is nothing "wrong" with not knowing what to do. This experience happens to everyone, and ultimately it teaches each of us new things about the way the world works.

PREPARING FOR ACTION

It is important to remember not only that problems are solvable, but also, as stated before, that many possibilities for action exist in any situation. Creative solutions often come from people who are unfamiliar with the intricacies of the issue and have an outsider's perspective.

When a process politician becomes too involved with a problem, he or she might decide to "opt out" temporarily by taking a short vacation or a leave of absence from the group in order to think. Sometimes it is most effective to retreat formally to gain a new perspective and to prepare oneself for taking action.

DECIDING WHAT TO DO

After one begins to think positively, he or she finds exciting new possibilities. Attitude makes a great difference in one's ability to find creative answers to problems.

There are many specific ways to go about developing new strategies. In addition, strategies can be developed by an individual or by an entire group. In either case, an open approach that relies on feelings, hunches, and a diversity of opinions is helpful.

Mike, a process politician, demonstrated the value of involving a group in establishing strategies. Each member first wrote a personal list of alternative actions, placing a premium on quantity. The lists were shared in the group, each person explaining one idea at a time. This process continued until all ideas had been shared. Some of the strategies were funny, some were realistic, and some were ridiculous. Ultimately, the group had a pool of over 130 alternatives.

Brainstorming generates ideas from which to choose. Such a list might be developed by group members working together at a meeting or through phone contacts between individual members. In addition, a suggestion box may be used, or various people may be polled. The particular approach used by a group depends on the time and energy that its members can spend.

When there is little time for figuring out what to do, there is even less time for worrying and spinning one's wheels. Sometimes this situation is for the best anyway.

Eileen was asked to facilitate a group meeting in which there was conflict. She started the session by letting the members know that she had no plan. Together they figured out what to do and relied on their collective intuition to work things out.

A process politician should not be afraid to act on hunches; these hunches are usually right.

It is helpful to write down what is happening during a meeting as well as what should happen next. Writing forces a person to sort out thoughts and to make connections between them. This practice is especially useful when one has not had a chance to analyze the situation carefully. The person who writes down thoughts before saying them is able to be more articulate, especially about controversial topics.

Other strategies include the following:

- Hiring a consultant;
- Asking new people to help and to share the burden of the work;
- Going with the group on a weekend outing or to lunch in order to achieve a fresh perspective;
- Withdrawing from the situation by quitting the group or lowering resistance;
- Allowing the project at hand to be a failure (in accordance with the assumption that people are not able to experience success unless they are free to fail); and
- Reading about the experiences of others in similar situations.

Learning how to get around not knowing what to do serves a dual function. Knowing that there is a way out of the "foxhole" can keep a process politician from becoming trapped there in the first place. The more one thinks in terms of possibilities instead of limitations, the fewer "dead ends" are encountered; once the basic tools for figuring out what to do have been grasped, many solutions can be created.

RELATED READINGS

Glasser, W. *Positive addiction.* New York: Harper & Row, 1976.

Pearce, J.C. *Magical child: Rediscovery of nature's plan for our children.* New York: E.P. Dutton, 1975.

CHAPTER 11

GROUP EFFECTIVENESS
AND SOCIAL CHANGE

The arena of process politics encompasses many interacting individuals and groups, each with its own set of motivators, goals, and values. As these variables become more complex, the importance of the process politician increases.

It is easy for a process politician to become frustrated when working to bring about change within an organization; the frustration is compounded when he or she becomes involved with change that crosses organizational boundaries. Long-term change must be approached one step at a time if it is to work.

The key to bringing about long-term change when multiple groups and subgroups are involved is to pay attention to self-interest issues at all levels and to be aware of power dynamics among the various groups. This is no easy matter. The complexity of dynamics when numerous individuals, groups, organizations, systems, or networks are involved can be overwhelming, especially if the self-interests involved are in direct opposition or are not explicitly acknowledged. The concepts of process politics can be very useful in analyzing these complicated issues and in developing strategies that lead toward change.

SYSTEMS AND THEIR VALUES

A system is a collection of groups that possess common interests around which they have structured themselves. As a system becomes larger, personal beliefs and values are expressed less often, and individuals feel less personally involved. More compromises are needed among the competing self-interests in order to achieve a concerted action within the system. At the same time, the system takes on its own identity, independent of the individuals who are in leadership roles or the groups that comprise it. The system itself becomes the focal point, rather than individual members' needs and self-interests.

Internal energy and resources are called on to fulfill system goals, even when this commitment requires individuals to act contrary to their personal values or beliefs.

A major city hospital was faced with increasing pressure from government and the insurance industry to cut costs. Despite personal priorities regarding patient services, nursing supervisors found themselves spending more and more time in meetings concerned with fiscal management and third-party reimbursement mechanisms.

Over time the values of a system become formalized and take on a life of their own. They become institutionalized, and a principal mission of the evolving institution becomes self-perpetuation. In an institution individual values are, by definition, less important than institutional values—those that maintain the system.

As a system evolves to become an institution, decision-making responsibility becomes obscured, and individuals experience a growing sense of alienation and apathy. Paperwork mounts, and documentation becomes the byword. Conformity in dress and in operating procedure is demanded more and more, with people being ostracized or transferred if they threaten the institutional values.

Unwritten institutional values determine the priorities and the behavior of the institution, whether the values agree with the official mission statement of the organization or not. This adds a new dimension of complexity to the process of change—institutional self-interest.

The key to influencing change in systems is to find people within the system who feel that their personal needs and interests are being hampered by the system. Some ways to recognize when systemic values are the issue are as follows:

- The behavior within the system is at odds with the stated purposes of the system.
- Despite good intentions, the needs of individuals are frustrated by the system's demands for orderliness and accountability.
- It is difficult to find out who makes decisions.
- People frequently use words like "they" and "them," suggesting strong feelings of powerlessness about their situations, whether chosen or imposed.
- Most available resources are used for maintaining information systems; very few resources are devoted to people.

- There is increasing pressure to conform to prescribed dress codes and behavior patterns.
- Phrases such as "That's the way it has always been done" are often heard, suggesting the influence of tradition within the system.

Making change in the context of a system or institution is an immense challenge, especially if the specific issue requires change in institutional values. The situation of the hospital mentioned previously is a good example.

As the hospital's value of cost-effective care at the expense of quality care became more widely felt among the nursing staff, the nurses' morale plummeted and complaints from both staff members and patients increased. No one had any answers about how to resolve the dilemma, but everyone (including top administrators) blamed "them."

Changing institutional values requires a major commitment in time and energy on the part of individuals throughout the system. However, when these individuals share a desire to challenge the institutional values and to meet their own needs more effectively, this common interest can form the basis for building a new power base within the system, a power base whose very presence jars the existing balance of power.

A MODEL FOR UNDERSTANDING POWER IN SYSTEMS

One way to develop an understanding of the internal workings of systems is to construct a mobile to represent a system. At the top there is a framework from which all the rest is suspended. Each group is represented by larger pieces, to which may be attached smaller parts representing subgroups and individual members. Some groups are directly connected to the superstructure or to other groups, while other connections between components may be less apparent.

The key to a mobile is *balance:* The stability of one branch is dependent on the existence of stable conditions throughout. Just as one piece of the mobile cannot be added or moved without making an impact on the whole mobile, any change in a group has an impact on the whole system.

If there is a change in the balance of power within a system, the whole system gets out of balance. In order to regain balance, new power relationships must be identified and formalized.

The relative power of any group in a system greatly influences that group's view of issues and priorities. The Power Lab provides some categories that illustrate how power differences can affect an individual's or a group's perception of reality (Oshry, 1975).

1. *Powerful Ins*, the power elite, tend to see the system's needs in broad perspectives. Their constituency is the system itself. They tend to perceive the needs of individuals and groups as less important than the needs of the existing system. Because their power in the system is dependent on maintaining the status quo, they tend to resist change in institutional values. Regardless of their motives, Powerful Ins are pulled between long-range concerns on one hand and group and individual needs on the other. As a result the decisions they make take time and frequently involve difficult choices.

2. *Powerless Ins*, the support people, rely on their skills and their personal contacts to exert influence in a system. The power they have lies in their knowledge of the needs of various groups within the system. By helping these groups articulate their concerns, they can strengthen the building blocks of systemic change. Systems are complex, and the temptation is strong for Powerless Ins to deal with symptoms rather than causes of problems. People's immediate needs are important, but so are the larger systemic issues that cause these needs to exist.

3. *Powerless Outs*, members of groups with no political clout, are not included in the decision-making processes of the system, even though they may be directly affected by those decisions. Re-

gardless of whether Powerless Outs are "out" by choice, by active exclusion, or by tradition, the feeling of powerlessness they experience is real. They can see every day that they have less than other groups in the system. Yet without the skills, confidence, or status to successfully enter into negotiations with the Powerful Ins, they may give up and resign themselves to a less-than-equal share, focusing their change efforts on immediate, short-term, individual issues.

The Powerless Outs do have some forms of power, but unless those forms are built on and strengthened, the group will not be able to effectively use its power. The power of the Powerless Outs lies in the unifying force of their common condition. It is this unity that can be harnessed for their mutual benefit.

Alinsky (1971) developed his community-organization model by finding ways to harness the energy of the Powerless Outs to effect change. Organizers of these efforts are often members of the Powerless In group, who apply their skills to deal with the oppression of

Powerless Outs are not just the poor or members of minority groups. Many segments of institutional or organizational society also perceive themselves as being powerless. Whether the lack of power is real or perceived, the feeling of powerlessness and alienation is what needs to be recognized. Groups who feel powerless *are* powerless unless something happens to show them otherwise.

A factor that interferes with the ability of Powerless Outs to turn their situation around is the fear of losing what little they already have. They already feel victimized, and experience has shown them that it is generally safer to keep quiet.

> The Power Lab model demonstrates that groups and systems exist in relation to each other. Every system is connected to other systems in a wide variety of ways. The mobile used to picture a system is really part of a larger mobile in which all the parts are intricately interconnected. This larger context has groups and systems with a vast array of interdependent institutional values and power relationships. This is the setting for long-range change.

REFERENCES

Alinsky, S. *Rules for radicals.* New York: Random House, 1971.

Oshry, B. Power and the Power Lab. In W.W. Burke (Ed.), *New technologies in organization development: 1.* San Diego, CA: University Associates, 1975.

RELATED READINGS

Bateson, G. *Steps to an ecology of mind.* New York: Ballantine, 1975.

Knowles, L., & Prewitt, K. *Institutional racism in America.* Englewood Cliffs, NJ: Prentice-Hall, 1969.

Schein, E.H. *Organizational psychology.* Englewood Cliffs, NJ: Prentice-Hall, 1965.

PART III

PROCESS POLITICS: APPLICATIONS

Chapter 12 offers suggestions of specific areas to which process politics can be applied: on the job, in voluntary organizations, at the neighborhood level, and at policy-making levels. In addition, it presents a discussion of the question of ethics in using the principles of process politics and concludes with an emphasis on the importance of nonrational aspects of managing change.

SUGGESTIONS FOR THE APPLICATION OF PROCESS POLITICS

This book does not attempt to prescribe the exact issues to which the concepts and methods of process politics can be applied. Because these methods can be applied in any situation in which a group is working toward its members' common goals, all task-oriented groups can benefit from using them.

Process politics is political, not because it is applied to specific "political" issues, but rather because process politicians attempt to influence groups toward effective processes of cooperative problem solving and collaborative action. A group may have political goals (such as increasing opportunities for women in management or improving municipal services), or it may have a planning function (such as designing a new church structure or developing a new product line). The point is that whatever the goals, process politics can help a group to achieve success.

SPECIFIC AREAS OF APPLICATION

On the Job

One starting point for applying process politics is at work. People from various fields are exploring options for making the most of work for both management and nonmanagement personnel. Ideas being considered include the following:

- *Flexible scheduling,* which permits employees a degree of freedom in scheduling their working time in order to minimize time conflicts and to allow for individual preferences;
- *Shared positions* in which two people each work part-time, sharing a full-time job;

- *Stress-management training* to help employees at all levels learn skills to minimize the negative effects of job pressures; and
- *Industrial wellness programs*, in which employees are provided with accurate information about current health problems, assessments of the health risks involved with their life styles, and opportunities to learn new skills to minimize health risks.

Cooperative and collaborative management styles are used in many types of organizations, including businesses, service agencies, educational institutions, religious groups, and community programs. Growing numbers of organizations are discovering that when employees feel significantly involved in solving problems and suggesting ideas, there are payoffs in productivity as well as employee satisfaction.

There are many ways to become involved in process politics on the job. Although it is easier to do so when the employer invites and provides a structure for employee ideas and suggestions, it is possible even without organizational support. In either case it is important to remember that most people—especially those who are one's superiors in a hierarchical structure—do not respond favorably to attempts to force them to change. Self-interest is the key to changing behavior, and building strategies for change around self-interest issues is usually more effective and more lasting.

Opportunities to apply process politics on the job may start with any of the following activities:

- Posting information on bulletin boards to help people understand an issue;
- Giving visibility to effective work-style behaviors in the organization through word of mouth, memorandums, posters, and so forth;
- Seeking information about advisory-committee and task-force opportunities to solve problems or to develop plans; and
- Making use of a suggestion box.

Whether one functions as an internal or an external change agent, the challenge of helping to develop fulfilling management and decision-making styles within a work setting is exciting. It is always better to take the initiative to make changes than to grumble about an unsatisfactory situation.

In Voluntary Organizations

Many people belong to groups or organizations in which their participation is voluntary, such as fire departments, church auxiliaries, or boards of directors. People join these organizations because of shared interests or goals. It is sometimes difficult for people to see any self-interests in relation to their participation in voluntary organizations, especially in ones that are service oriented. Yet it is extremely important to recognize the need for nonfinancial rewards for volunteers.

Members of voluntary organizations will stay active if their involvement meets their needs. They may want to feel useful, they may want to learn new skills, or they may want to have opportunities to interact with others in a productive way. What is essential is that members acknowledge to one another the needs that they have and help each other achieve those personal rewards. For example, a member might want to learn to speak out more often, to conduct a good meeting, or to handle conflict more appropriately. If other group members are aware of such interests, opportunities can be created to support these types of learning and to increase the skills available within the group.

Most voluntary organizations have a variety of committees or subgroups that offer opportunities for member involvement in activities ranging from planning to program development to fund raising. There is usually no lack of opportunity to practice process politics in these groups. All that is required is a willingness to volunteer.

At the Neighborhood Level

Neighborhoods are in many ways microcosms of larger society. Individuals, organizations, systems, groups, and institutions from all sectors interact daily at the neighborhood level as they carry out activities related to survival and fulfillment. Much of this interaction is invisible and taken for granted, yet grass-roots involvement is an ideal context in which to think about and apply the leadership-development aspects of process politics.

The role of the process politician in a neighborhood is often that of a behind-the-scenes personality who functions as an educator, advocate, and support person. This role also involves becoming active in task groups as they come into being and as they adapt to changing needs. It is important for neighborhood-based process politicians to help groups look at their decision-making processes and develop effective leadership styles. For example, simply talking informally with a block-club member about how a meeting went can acknowledge that person's worth as well as his or her continuing participation and learning. It is useful to remember that many elected officials, civic leaders, and professional managers get their starts in their own neighborhoods, working on issues directly affecting their day-to-day lives.

Applying process politics in neighborhoods requires a high degree of patience and a solid base of personal support. Neighborhood-group members devote their time on a voluntary basis only; in addition, they often lack the experience, knowledge, and skills associated with being effective group members. On the other hand, the rewards are gratifying for a process politician who, over time, watches people gain confidence and expertise and move into other leadership positions in the community and on the job.

Some of the entry points for potential leaders in neighborhood activities are as follows:

- block clubs and community organizations
- community-development corporations
- political precinct clubs
- community-education programs
- neighborhood advisory boards
- cooperatively owned businesses

The subject matters that are covered by such groups range from crime prevention to housing rehabilitation, economic development, and energy concerns. Involvement in neighborhoods, where participants come from such varied perspectives and backgrounds, can lead to exciting opportunities for creative problem solving and the development of new models for interdisciplinary cooperation and win/win solutions.

At Policy-Making Levels

There are many opportunities for consumers of services to have a say in determining the shape of those services. Participation of low- and moderate-income people in decision making has expanded into many fields; boards and commissions that formerly consisted only of "blue-ribbon" names now often include a cross section of representatives from private, government, and community sectors.

Public-interest groups often act as watchdogs to ensure that consumers have strong representation on advisory bodies and national study commissions. But responsibility for monitoring trends and advocating citizen concerns does not rest with "someone else." Each of us shares that responsibility; and, if we choose to take part, we can all help to develop ideas for solving the problems currently facing us as a society.

The person who is interested in learning about ways to directly influence decisions in such fields as health care, the environment, or urban areas can easily start by contacting his or her congressperson's office to obtain advice on how to proceed. Part of an elected official's job is to help his or her constituents understand how decisions are made and how they can have access to those decision-making processes.

Involvement in an advisory committee or a study commission includes taking the initiative for obtaining the information, training, and technical assistance necessary to be effective. It is a good idea to insist on an orientation period that encompasses *maintenance issues*, such as how the meetings will be run and where they will be held to promote full participation, as well as *technical concerns*, such as whose job it is to implement the group's recommendations and which government regulations govern the group's focus area. Individual members should be encouraged to express their opinions regarding the group's progress. This practice not only provides an opportunity for the group to take action to avoid trouble spots; it also fosters group self-awareness and ownership of decisions.

THE QUESTION OF ETHICS

If there is a code of ethics for process politicians, it has to do with the uses and abuses of power. Effective process politicians are powerful. They have access to information about issues and people, and they are influential in determining who obtains that information and how it is used.

As emphasized previously, power, in and of itself, is neither good nor bad. We all have choices to make about taking or not taking power in our own lives, and we have further choices to make about ways to use that power once we have it. In the context of process politics, appropriate uses of power are those that enhance the ability of other people to use their own power, whereas inappropriate uses of power keep people in dependent relationships.

It is important to establish an accountability mechanism to help keep perspective and to avoid misusing power. This type of mechanism works in much the same way as the system of checks and balances that limits Congress, the President, and the judicial system. One way in which a process politician can monitor personal power is to ask his or her support group and/or constituents to help in this respect. Such people should be encouraged to express their thoughts, to share their ideas about how to make things better, and to provide feedback about the way in which the process politician is functioning. In turn, the process politician should listen to their ideas and assure these people that their comments and criticisms are considered valuable and welcome. It is of utmost importance for process politicians to be conscious of how they are using their power by periodically taking time to assess the impact of their behaviors.

A significant barrier to effective change is greed. Greed occurs at all levels of functioning, from the personal to the institutional, and it causes people to take action based on narrow and limited concepts of self-interest. Process politics builds in some controls on personal greed with its value on long-range perspectives and broad-based involvement in decision making. It is important for process politicians to remind groups frequently of their missions and of these values as a way to discourage parochialism and to encourage win/win approaches to problem solving.

Losing on a particular issue is no justification for abandoning win/win models for change. All of us experience times when we lose. What is important is to be able to acknowledge our efforts, to identify where we went wrong, and to learn from our mistakes as well as our successes. No matter what the outcome, the process of trying to bring about change within a system disrupts the status quo, increases people's knowledge and skills, and impacts the balance of power. There may be retrenching and backlash as immediate repercussions, but the learning that takes place during such a process can ultimately lead to win/win solutions that are permanent.

NONRATIONAL ASPECTS OF MANAGING CHANGE

Process politics has been presented as a set of assumptions and techniques to help group members to manage their own growth and development toward becoming capable problem solvers. It works through encouraging personal and group self-awareness, and it creates activities that have the support of group members because their concerns are considered in all aspects of group functioning.

The concepts of process politics are built primarily on rational, logical, analytical ways of thinking about change. Only occasional mention has been made of such nonrational, intuitive ways of thinking as trusting hunches; but the lack of attention in this book to nonrational processes does not mean that they are unimportant. Intuition (or psychic insight) is an important part of being effective in any setting; rational processes are often too ponderous to allow for sorting through the complexities of individual and group concerns quickly enough to make a timely intervention.

> One group leader often sensed some new dynamic in the group that suggested an intervention to facilitate progress. Whenever this circumstance occurred, the leader tried to figure out logically what was taking place and then choose an appropriate intervention. Meanwhile, the group continued working. Often, however, another group member said what the leader had been thinking first; and the leader could only respond with "That's just what I was thinking." By not trusting and acting on intuitional insights, the leader missed many opportunities to help the group.

The purpose here is merely to point to the importance of nonrational ways of enhancing personal and group effectiveness. Although some people seem naturally adept at promoting insights at the proper time, anyone can develop this ability. Many methods can be used to train intuition and to develop nonrational skills, including mind-control techniques, language restructuring, visualization, meditation, hypnosis, and altering consciousness through various means. One of the authors uses the concept of managing human energy to develop nonrational awareness and skills.

By training intuition and acknowledging the full range of human potential, we can perceive that rational, conscious forces are always interacting with nonrational, unconscious realities. Change in one accompanies change in the other, and change can be managed on both levels. Effective process politicians find ways to use both rational and nonrational approaches to managing change.

The opportunities for employing the principles of process politics are many. Positive group change can be instituted in an atmosphere in which members are able to express their individual needs and assist each other in achieving personal as well as group goals. In several different facets— on the job, in voluntary organizations, at the neighborhood level, and at policy-making levels—people who are committed to helping their groups function more effectively can do so by emphasizing cooperation and collaboration and by building strategies for change around self-interest issues. The process politician as change agent can help group members examine their decision-making processes, adopt effective leadership styles, avoid trouble spots, explore opportunities for creative problem solving, develop self-awareness and ownership of decisions, and find new ways to effect win/win solutions. Ultimately, through the appropriate use of power, the process politician can foster the abilities of other people to use their own power.

APPENDIX

The Appendix consists of a set of five maintenance checks for the use of group members who wish to increase their understanding of the internal dynamics of their groups. These checks, one of which was presented in simplified form in Chapter 5, serve as tools to "diagnose" a group's health. Following the maintenance checks is a list of recommended readings that might prove both useful and interesting. For the reader's convenience, this list is presented in categories: change in organizations, change in communities, humanism and human relations, issues and perspectives, and consciousness.

MAINTENANCE CHECKS

Each of the five maintenance checks that follow [14] includes five steps and can be completed in approximately forty minutes. It is recommended that they be done in the order in which they are presented.

MAINTENANCE CHECK 1: MEMBERSHIP

Step 1: Each group member silently reads the following paragraphs and reflects on the questions and his or her membership role in the group.

As individuals become members of groups, they tend to concern themselves at first with the nature of their membership. Individuals identified as being parts of the group are said to have membership. At the level of the individual, membership applies to issues of a person's self-identity. It speaks to questions such as these:

1. Who am I?
2. What can I be?
3. What do I expect and desire of myself?

For more complex levels of group behavior, it speaks to such questions as the following:

1. What does it mean to be a member of this group, organization, community, or society?
2. Will I be accepted?
3. How will I be expected to act and respond?

---

[14]Adapted from a set of "maintenance checks" developed by David Goodlow for use at the Regional Training Center in Minneapolis, Minnesota, in 1972. The checks are drawn from materials developed in part by the Northwest Regional Educational Laboratory in Portland, Oregon. Used with permission.

4. What norms will prevail?
5. Will I be trusted?
6. Will I feel satisfied that I am needed and respected?
7. Will I feel adequate?
8. Will my personal motivations fit in with those of the group?
9. How much freedom will I have to express myself?

Step 2: The group spends some time in discussion as the individual members contribute answers to this question: In what ways have I seen some of these concerns raised in my experiences in *other* groups (not this group)? Everyone tries to adhere to this topic as much as possible.

Step 3: Each group member completes the following questionnaire by circling the appropriate number on each line.

1. How clear am I about my membership role?

1	2	3	4	5
Confused				Clear

2. Do I feel that I am accepted on an equal basis with others in the group?

1	2	3	4	5
Unaccepted				Fully accepted

3. Am I able to converse in my accustomed manner when I am in this group?

1	2	3	4	5
Never				Always

5. Do I understand what this group expects of me?

1	2	3	4	5
Do not understand				Fully understand

6. Do I feel trusted by the others in this group?

1	2	3	4	5
Not at all				Totally

7. Do I feel comfortable while working in this group?

1	2	3	4	5

Uncomfortable   Very comfortable

8. Am I expected to give up my values, beliefs, and motivations?

1	2	3	4	5

Totally   Not at all

9. Am I committed to being an effective member of this group?

1	2	3	4	5

Uncommitted   Fully committed

Step 4: The members record the results of their questionnaires on a grid form. Each member retains a record of all responses. No discussion takes place during this step.

Group Member

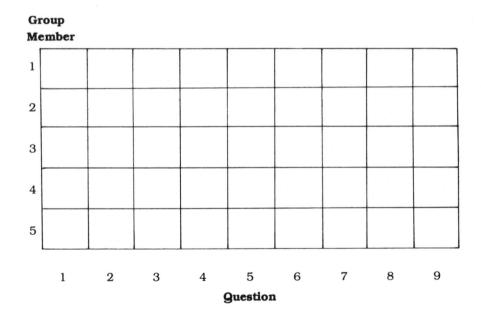

Step 5: The results of the data from step 4 are discussed, but individual members do not defend their answers. Each member tries to understand and be clear about what he or she as well as

the others are feeling. (All members try to help the group observe these guidelines.)

MAINTENANCE CHECK 2: INFLUENCE

Step 1: Each group member silently reads the following paragraphs and reflects on the questions and his or her influence role in the group.

As membership concerns begin to clear, questions arise in a group concerning the flow of influence between and among the group members. Influence can be defined in terms of control, manipulation, or facilitation. Control can be considered at one end of a spectrum of choice, facilitation at the other.

Control	**Manipulate**	**Facilitate**
One Choice	Few Choices	Increased Choices

Influence questions center around the manner in which one influences or is influenced and the member who influences or is influenced. Examples are as follows:

1. Who is the leader in the group?
2. Does the leadership vary with concerns?
3. How are decisions made?
4. Are the members having "power struggles"?
5. Are the members open to being influenced, or are they resistant? Are they "counterdependent"—resisting because of a need *not* to be influenced?
6. What opportunities are there for each member to exercise leadership or influence?
7. Are there individuals in the group who care more about the power of being leaders than they do about the goals and issues of the group?
8. Is influence used by exerting the power of "experience" or "knowledge" or "emotional commitment"?
9. Are the members' outside roles being used to influence the group? If some members have roles that imply expertise in certain areas, is that expertise used to control the decisions of the group?

When the group deals effectively with these influence concerns, each member feels more committed to the group's decisions and the implementation of goals is more effective. At this point each group member should consider what problems the group may have concerning control, manipulation, and facilitation.

Step 2: The group spends some time in discussion as the individual members contribute answers to this question: In what ways have I seen some of these concerns raised in my experience in this group? Everyone tries to adhere to this topic as much as possible.

Step 3: Each group member completes the following questionnaire by circling the appropriate number on each line.

1. Do I tend to decrease or increase the choices of others by control, manipulation, or facilitation?

1	2	3	4	5
Decrease				Increase

2. Do I feel controlled, manipulated, or facilitated by one or more members of the group?

1	2	3	4	5
Controlled (members decrease my choices)		Manipulated (members restrict my choices)		Facilitated (members increase my choices)

3. Is leadership controlled, or does it vary with the concerns or tasks of the group?

1	2	3	4	5
Controlled— always the same person				Varied— most take leadership at different times

4. How are decisions usually made in the group?

1	2	3	4	5
Vote—power struggles				Consensus

5. Do I tend to be open to alternative solutions, or do I usually have an opinion that is set at the beginning?

1	2	3	4	5

Set opinions—   Open to many
difficult to change   alternatives

6. Is the group open to and searching for alternatives, or is it usually locked in struggles between members with set ideas?

1	2	3	4	5

Locked in struggles—   Open to
set ideas   alternatives

7. Does the group have members who use their outside roles to unduly influence the direction of the group?

1	2	3	4	5

Roles used   Everyone exerts
to exert undue   influence without
influence   undue reference
                                                       to outside roles

Step 4: The members record the results of their questionnaires on a grid form. Each member retains a record of all responses. No discussion takes place during this step.

Step 5: The results of the data from step 4 are discussed, but individual members do not defend their answers. Each member tries to understand and be clear about what he or she as well as the others are feeling. (All members try to help the group observe these guidelines.)

MAINTENANCE CHECK 3: FEELINGS

Step 1: Each group member silently reads the following paragraphs and reflects on the questions and his or her role in the group.

Perhaps the most crucial contribution of psychology in the past few decades has been clarification of the ways in which feelings affect the operations of groups. They can affect any and all functions in facilitative and blocking ways. Feelings are tangible, measurable, and enduring. Those that are not expressed as they occur are frequently expressed later in disguised, inappropriate, and obstructive ways. Questions such as these are important:

1. What are acceptable and unacceptable ways of expressing different kinds of feelings in this group?
2. Are there any kinds of feelings for which there is no acceptable means of expression?
3. Do the members trust each other?
4. What are the characteristic ways in which less acceptable feelings show themselves, and how obstructive are these manifestations?
5. How much variance in individual styles of expressing feelings is tolerated?
6. How spontaneous, open, and direct are expressions of feelings?
7. Is the importance of the expression of feelings accepted?

Problems arise most frequently from lack of clarity about feelings. They can also stem from conflict over the ways in which feelings are expressed. At this point each member should reflect on these questions and his or her role in the group.

Step 2: The group spends some time in discussion as the individual members contribute answers to this question: In what ways have I seen some of these concerns raised in my experience in this group? Everyone tries to adhere to this topic as much as possible.

Step 3: Each member completes the following questionnaire by circling the appropriate number on each line.

1. The way I express myself in this group is acceptable.

1	2	3	4	5
Never				Always

2. There are some feelings that I have trouble sharing in this group.

1	2	3	4	5
Seldom				Often

3. I feel trusted in this group.

1	2	3	4	5
Never				Always

4. I feel that unacceptable feelings in this group are obstructive.

1	2	3	4	5

Seldom   Often

5. I am open and direct when expressing my feelings in this group.

1	2	3	4	5

Never   Always

6. I feel that the acceptance of expression of feelings is important in this group.

1	2	3	4	5

Never   Always

Step 4: The members record the results of their questionnaires on a grid form. Each member retains a record of all responses. No discussion takes place during this step.

Step 5: The results of the data from step 4 are discussed, but individual members do not defend their answers. Each member tries to understand and be clear about what he or she as well as the others are feeling. (All members try to help the group observe these guidelines.)

MAINTENANCE CHECK 4: COMMUNICATIONS

Step 1: Each group member silently reads the following paragraphs and reflects on the questions.

As a group clarifies its membership, its influence, and its approach to feelings, it begins to concern itself with communication issues. Questions arise that deal with norms about the manner in which concerns are dealt with by the group or by individuals. The term "information" as it is used in the following questions applies to news items. There may be other types of information being discussed that seem to be unintelligible or redundant "noise." Such noise usually distorts, rather than aids, the passage of information about news items. These are some of the important questions regarding group communication:

1. Who talks to whom about what?

2. What modes and personal styles of communication are unacceptable or acceptable in the group?
3. How efficient are communications in terms of information flow versus noise and redundancy?
4. Do the members provide feedback of information, checking for understanding, and opportunities for two-way flow when needed?
5. Are formal and informal patterns of communication primarily functional rather than bound by tradition and conflicts or limited by assumptions?
6. How do norms, roles, expectations, and feelings influence communications?
7. Are there bottlenecks, blocks, gaps, or points of overload in the lines of communication?

The pattern that a group selects as the norm for its communication either helps or hinders the group's effectiveness. At this point each member should reflect on these questions and his or her role in the group.

Step 2: The group spends some time in discussion as the individual members contribute answers to this question: In what ways have I seen some of these concerns raised in my experience in this group? Everyone tries to adhere to this topic as much as possible.

Step 3: Each member completes the following questionnaire by circling the appropriate number on each line.

1. Am I able to say what I think or what I feel?

1	2	3	4	5
Never				Always

2. Am I listened to by the group?

1	2	3	4	5
Never				Always

3. Do I feel interrupted or cut off by others?

1	2	3	4	5
Never				Always

4. Do I feel controlled by others?

1	2	3	4	5
Never				Always

5. Do I block others so that they cannot fully express themselves?

1	2	3	4	5
Never				Always

6. I receive and understand feedback.

1	2	3	4	5
Never				Always

7. I give feedback to others.

1	2	3	4	5
Never				Always

Step 4: The members record the results of their questionnaires on a grid form. Each member retains a record of all responses. No discussion takes place during this step.

Step 5: The results of the data from step 4 are discussed, but individual members do not defend their answers. Each member tries to understand and be clear about what he or she as well as the others are feeling. (All members try to help the group observe these guidelines.)

MAINTENANCE CHECK 5: INDIVIDUAL DIFFERENCES

Step 1: Each group member silently reads the following paragraphs and reflects on the questions and his or her role in the group.

Each member of a group represents certain unique experiences, knowledge, and skills. Few groups seem to reach a point at which they take maximum advantage of these individual differences. It is rather common for members of a group to reach a level of sharing feelings at which each sees the others as likeable because they seem to be the same as he or she is. This is sometimes referred to as the "honeymoon stage." If enough trust develops, the members may begin to be able to both recognize and value the individual differences between them. A new set of questions then takes on meaning.

1. Do the members take the time and effort to learn about the experiences, attitudes, knowledge, values, skills, and ideologies of each other?

2. Does each member work at sharing his or her own ideas in order to obtain others' reactions and different ways of looking at issues?

3. Do the members let each other know that they appreciate these differences when they do not necessarily agree with them?

4. Is appreciation of these differences merely an acceptance that there are differences, or is it an attempt to find the commonalities behind those differences as well as a feeling of deep understanding that such differences can add to the effectiveness of the group if understood?

5. Are the members different just to be different, or do they look for similarities of opinion and allow the differences to create new insights and understandings about each other?

Groups have a tendency to attempt to level out their differences or to polarize around them to form power factions. As groups are able to deal with individual differences, they tend to find new resources for their effectiveness.

Step 2: The group spends some time in discussion as the individual members contribute answers to this question: In what ways have I seen some of these concerns raised in my experience in this group? Everyone tries to adhere to this topic as much as possible.

Step 3: Each member completes the following questionnaire by circling the appropriate number on each line.

1. Are feelings expressed openly so that differences become apparent in the group?

1	2	3	4	5

No expression of
feelings, or feelings
expressed inappropriately

Open expression of
feelings—appropriate
indication of what
each member
is experiencing

2. Do members of the group discuss and understand the values, beliefs, attitudes, and so forth of each member?

1	2	3	4	5

Not discussed
or understood

Discussed and
understood clearly

3. Have I shared my values, beliefs, attitudes, and so forth with this group?

1	2	3	4	5

Not shared at all

Shared openly

4. Do I feel concerned about the values, beliefs, attitudes, behavior, and so forth of other group members?

1	2	3	4	5

Very concerned

Appreciative
of differences,
but not concerned

5. Does the group understand my uniqueness and accept me for it?

1	2	3	4	5

Does not understand
or accept

Understands and
accepts

6. Do members of the group feel unity among themselves apart from their ability to work on tasks together?

1	2	3	4	5

No feeling of unity
except when
working on tasks

Common areas
understood

7. Do the group members attempt to influence each other to be and think alike in most respects?

1	2	3	4	5

Attempt to
influence thinking
and behavior

Allow each other
to think and be
what they wish

8. Do I feel pressure to give up what I think, believe, and do?

1	2	3	4	5

Great pressure   No pressure

Step 4: The members record the results of their questionnaires on a grid form. Each member retains a record of all responses. No discussion takes place during this step.

Step 5: The results of the data from step 4 are discussed, but individual members do not defend their answers. Each member tries to understand and be clear about what he or she as well as the others are feeling. (All members try to help the group observe these guidelines.)

RECOMMENDED READINGS

CHANGE IN ORGANIZATIONS

Argyris, C. *The applicability of organizational sociology.* Cambridge, MA: University Press, 1972.

Argyris, C. *Integrating the individual and the organization.* New York: John Wiley, 1964.

Argyris, C. *Intervention theory and method.* Reading, MA: Addison-Wesley, 1970.

Beckhard, R. *Organization development: Strategies and models.* Reading, MA: Addison-Wesley, 1969. (Addison-Wesley series on organization development.)

Bennis, W. *Changing organizations.* New York: McGraw-Hill, 1966.

Bennis, W. *Organization development: Its nature, origins, and prospects.* Reading, MA: Addison-Wesley, 1969. (Addison-Wesley series on organization development.)

Bennis, W., Benne, K., & Chin, R. *The planning of change.* New York: Holt, Rinehart and Winston, 1969.

Blake, R.R., & Mouton, J. *Building a dynamic corporation through grid organization development.* Reading, MA: Addison-Wesley, 1969. (Addison-Wesley series on organization development.)

Blake, R.R., & Mouton, J. *Corporate excellence through grid organization development.* Houston, TX: Gulf, 1968.

Blake, R.R., & Mouton, J.S. *The new managerial grid.* Houston, TX: Gulf, 1978.

Burke, W.W., & Beckhard, R. (Eds.). *Conference planning* (2nd ed.). San Diego, CA: University Associates, 1976.

Burns, J.M. *Leadership.* New York: Harper & Row, 1978.

Connors, T.D. (Ed.). *The nonprofit organization handbook.* New York: McGraw-Hill, 1980.

Cooper, S., & Heenan, C. *Preparing, designing, leading workshops: A humanistic approach.* Boston, MA: CBI Publishing, 1980.

Cummings, T.G., & Srivastva, S. *Management of work: A socio-technical systems approach.* San Diego, CA: University Associates, 1981.

Delbecq, A.L., Van de Ven, A.H., & Gustafson, D.H. *Group techniques for program planning: A guide to nominal group and Delphi processes.* Glenview, IL: Scott, Foresman, 1975.

Drucker, P. *Management: Tasks, responsibilities, practices.* New York: Harper & Row, 1974.

Eddy, W.B., & Burke, W.W. (Eds.). *Behavioral science and the manager's role* (2nd ed.). San Diego, CA: University Associates, 1980.

French, W., & Bell, C.H., Jr. *Organization development.* Englewood Cliffs, NJ: Prentice-Hall, 1973.

Golembiewski, R.T. *Approaches to planned change, part I: Orienting perspectives and micro-level interventions.* New York: Marcel Dekker, 1979.

Golembiewski, R.T. *Approaches to planned change, part II: Macro-level interventions and change-agent strategies.* New York: Marcel Dekker, 1979.

Havelock, R.G., & Havelock, M.C. *Training for change agents: A guide to the design of training programs in education and other fields.* Ann Arbor: University of Michigan, 1973.

Knudson, H.R., Woodworth, R., & Bell, C.H. *Management: Experiential approach.* New York: McGraw-Hill, 1973.

Kolb, D.A., Rubin, E.M., & McIntyre, J.M. *Organizational psychology: An experiential approach* (2nd ed.). Englewood Cliffs, NJ: Prentice-Hall, 1974.

Lawrence, P.R., & Lorsch, J.W. *Developing organizations: Diagnosis and action.* Reading, MA: Addison-Wesley, 1969. (Addison-Wesley series on organization development.)

Lippitt, G. *Organizational renewal.* New York: Appleton-Century-Crofts, 1969.

Lippitt, R., Watson, J., & Westley, B. *Dynamics of planned change: A comparative study of principles and techniques.* New York: Harcourt Brace Jovanovich, 1958.

McConkey, D.D. *MBO for nonprofit organizations.* New York: American Management Association, 1975.

Morrison, J.H. *The human side of management.* New York: Addison-Wesley, 1971.

Peter, L., & Hull, R. *The Peter principle.* New York: William Morrow, 1969.

Robinson, J.W., & Clifford, R.A. *Process skills in organization development.* Urbana: University of Illinois, Department of Agricultural Economics, 1972.

Rutman, L. *Planning useful evaluations.* Beverly Hills, CA: Sage, 1980.

Schein, E.H. *Organizational psychology.* Englewood Cliffs, NJ: Prentice-Hall, 1965.

Schein, E.H. *Process consultation.* Reading, MA: Addison-Wesley, 1969. (Addison-Wesley series on organization development.)

Schein, E., & Bennis, W. *Personal and organizational change through group methods.* New York: John Wiley, 1965.

Schindler-Rainman, E., & Lippitt, R. *Taking your meetings out of the doldrums.* San Diego, CA: University Associates, 1975.

Sheane, D. *Beyond bureaucracy: The future shape and transformation of large, complex organizations.* London: Management Research, 1976.

Steiner, R. *Managing the human service organization.* Beverly Hills, CA: Sage, 1977.

Townsend, R. *Up the organization.* Greenwich, CT: Fawcett Crest, 1970.

Van Maanen, J. *The process of program evaluation: A guide for managers.* Washington, DC: National Training and Development Service Press, 1973.

Walton, R.E. *Interpersonal peacemaking: Confrontations and third party consultation.* Reading, MA: Addison-Wesley, 1969.

Woodcock, M., & Francis, D. *Unblocking your organization.* San Diego, CA: University Associates, 1975.

CHANGE IN COMMUNITIES

Alinsky, S. *Reveille for radicals.* New York: Vintage, 1969.

Alinsky, S. *Rules for radicals.* New York: Random House, 1971.

Bradford, L.P. *Making meetings work: A guide for leaders and group members.* San Diego, CA: University Associates, 1976.

Cheever, J. *Your community and beyond: An information and action guide.* Palo Alto, CA: Page-Ficklin, 1975.

Cox, F.M. *Strategies of community organization.* Itasca, IL: F.E. Peacock, 1970.

Cox, F.M., Erlich, J.L., Rothman, J., & Tropman, J.E. (Eds.). *Community—action, planning, development: A casebook.* Itasca, IL: F.E. Peacock, 1974.

Cox, F.M., Erlich, J.L., Rothman, J., & Tropman, J.E. (Eds.). *Strategies of community organization: A book of readings.* Itasca, IL: F.E. Peacock, 1970.

Ecklein, J.L., & Lauffer, A.A. *Community organizers and social planners.* New York: John Wiley, 1972.

Evry, H. *The selling of a candidate.* Los Angeles: Western Opinion Research Center, 1971.

Fessler, D.R. *Facilitating community change: A basic guide.* San Diego, CA: University Associates, 1976.

Flanagan, J. *The grass roots fund raising book.* Chicago: Swallow Press, 1977.

Freire, P. *Pedagogy of the oppressed.* New York: Herder and Herder, 1972.

Grosser, C.F. *New directions in community organization.* New York: Holt, Rinehart and Winston, 1976.

Hallman, H.W. *Government by neighborhoods.* Washington, DC: Center for Governmental Studies, 1973.

Hallman, H.W. *The organization and operation of neighborhood councils.* New York: Praeger, 1977.

Hornstein, H.A. (Ed.). *Social intervention: A behavioral science analysis.* New York: Free Press, 1971.

Houle, C.O. *The effective board: A book designed to assist individuals who serve on boards of nonprofit agencies.* New York: Association Press, 1960.

Jones, M.H. *The autobiography of Mother Jones.* New York: Charles H. Kerr, 1972.

Kahn, S. *How people get power: Organizing oppressed communities for action.* New York: McGraw-Hill, 1970.

Klein, D.C. *Community dynamics and mental health.* New York: John Wiley, 1968.

Kotler, M. *Neighborhood government.* Indianapolis: Bobbs-Merrill, 1969.

Langton, S. (Ed.). *Citizen participation in America: Essays on the state of the art.* Lexington, MA: D.C. Heath, 1978.

Lauffer, A. *Social planning at the community level.* Englewood Cliffs, NJ: Prentice-Hall, 1978.

Littrell, D.W. *The theory and practice of community development: A guide for practitioners.* Columbia: Extension Division, University of Missouri—Columbia, 1974.

Mayer, R.R. *Social planning and social change.* Englewood Cliffs, NJ: Prentice-Hall, 1972.

Mitiguy, N. *The rich get richer and the poor write proposals.* Amherst: Citizen Involvement Training Project, University of Massachusetts, 1978.

Morris, D., Hess, K. *Neighborhood power: The new localism.* Boston, MA: Beacon Press, 1975.

Naylor, H.H. *Leadership for volunteering.* Dryden, NY: Dryden Associates, 1976.

Rothman, J. *Planning and organization for social change: Action principles from social science research.* New York: Columbia Press, 1974.

Schaller, L. *Community organization: Conflict and reconciliation.* Nashville, TN: Abingdon Press, 1966.

Schindler-Rainman, E., & Lippitt, R. *Taking your meetings out of the doldrums.* San Diego, CA: University Associates, 1975.

Simpson, D. *Winning elections.* Chicago: Swallow Press, 1976.

Simpson, D., & Beam, G. *Strategies for change: How to make the American political dream work.* Chicago: Swallow Press, 1972.

Spiegel, H.B.C. *Citizen participation in urban development* (Vols. I-3). San Diego, CA: University Associates, 1968, 1976, 1974.

Stevens Square design plan. Minneapolis, MN: Stevens Square Community Organization, 1976. (Can be obtained from Stevens Square Community Organization, 1725 Nicollet Avenue South, Minneapolis, MN 55403.)

Strauss, B., & Stowe, M.E. *How to get things changed.* Garden City, NY: Doubleday, 1974.

Warren, R.L. *The community in America.* Chicago: Rand McNally, 1978.

Warren, R.L. *Perspectives on the American community: A book of readings.* New York: Rand McNally, 1973.

Wellstone, P. *How the rural poor got power: Narrative of a grassroots organizer.* Amherst: University of Massachusetts Press, 1978.

Zaltman, G., Kotler, P., & Kaufman, I. (Eds.). *Creating social change.* New York: Holt, Rinehart and Winston, 1972.

HUMANISM AND HUMAN RELATIONS

Berne, E. *Games people play.* New York: Grove Press, 1964.

Bradford, L. *Making meetings work: A guide for leaders and group members.* San Diego, CA: University Associates, 1976.

Bradford, L., Gibb, J., & Benne, K. *T-group theory and laboratory method.* New York: John Wiley, 1965.

Dyer, W.W. *Your erroneous zones.* New York: T.Y. Crowell, 1976.

Fast, J. *Body language.* New York: Evans, 1970.

Filley, A.C. *Interpersonal conflict resolution.* Glenview, IL: Scott, Foresman, 1975.

Ford, D.L., Jr., *Readings in minority-group relations.* San Diego, CA: University Associates, 1976.

Golembiewski, R., & Blumberg, A. (Eds.). *Sensitivity training and the laboratory approach* (3rd ed.). Itasca, IL: F.E. Peacock, 1977.

Gordon, T. *Parent effectiveness training.* New York: Wyden Books, 1970.

Harris, T.A. *I'm ok—you're ok: A practical guide to transactional analysis.* New York: Harper & Row, 1969.

Henley, N.M. *Body politics: Power, sex, and nonverbal communication.* Englewood Cliffs, NJ: Prentice-Hall, 1977.

James, W. Humanism and truth. In *The works of William James.* Cambridge, MA: Harvard University Press, 1975.

Johnson, D.W. *Reaching out: Interpersonal effectiveness and self-actualization.* Englewood Cliffs, NJ: Prentice-Hall, 1972.

Laing, R.D. *The politics of experience.* New York: Pantheon Books, 1967.

Laing, R.D. *Self and others.* New York: Pantheon Books, 1970.

Maslow, A. *Toward a psychology of being.* New York: D. Van Nostrand, 1962.

Miller, S., Nunnally, E.W., & Wackman, D.B. *Alive and aware: How to improve your relationships through better communication.* Minneapolis, MN: Interpersonal Communication Programs, 1975.

Perls, F. *In and out the garbage pail.* Moab, UT: Real People Press, 1969.

Raths, L., Harmin, M., & Simon, S. *Values and teaching.* Columbus: Charles E. Merrill, 1966.

Rogers, C. *On becoming a person.* Boston, MA: Houghton Mifflin, 1961.

Satir, V. *Conjoint family therapy.* Palo Alto, CA: Science & Behavior Books, 1967.

Satir, V. *Making contact.* Millbrae, CA: Celestial Arts, 1976.

Satir, V. *Peoplemaking.* Palo Alto, CA: Science & Behavior Books, 1972.

Schutz, W. *Here comes everybody.* New York: Harper & Row, 1971.

Wackman, D.B., Miller, S., & Nunnally, E.W. *Student workbook: Increasing awareness and communication skills.* Minneapolis, MN: Interpersonal Communication Programs, 1977.

Watzlawick, P., Weakland, J.H., & Fisch, R. *Change: Principles of problem formation and problem resolution.* New York: W.W. Norton, 1974.

ISSUES AND PERSPECTIVES

Abuse. Minneapolis: University of Minnesota, 1973.

Albert, R., & Emmons, M. *Your perfect right.* San Luis Obispo, CA: Impact, 1975.

Baldwin, J. *Another country.* New York: Dial Press, 1962.

Beik, L.L. *Organizing for the integration of human services.* University Park: The Pennsylvania State University, 1977.

Bender, R. *Environmental design primer.* Denver, CO: Environmental Action Reprint Service, 1973.

Bolles, R.N. *What color is your parachute?* (5th rev. ed.). Berkeley, CA: Ten Speed Press, 1979.

Bradshaw, T.K., & Blakely, E.J. *Rural communities in advanced industrial society.* New York: Praeger, 1979.

Citizens' energy directory. Washington, DC: Citizens' Energy Project, 1979. (Can be obtained from Citizens' Energy Project, 1110 6th Street, NW, Washington, DC 20001.)

Commoner, B. *The closing circle.* New York: Alfred A. Knopf, 1971.

Conner, D.M. *Citizens participate: An action guide for public issues.* Oakville, Ontario: Development Publications, 1974. (Can be obtained from Development Publications Ltd., P.O. Box 84, Postal Station A, Willowdale, Ontario M2N 5S7, Canada.)

Cox, H. *The secular city.* New York: Macmillan, 1966.

Deloria, V., Jr. *Behind the trail of broken treaties.* New York: Dell, 1974.

DeRivera, J. *Field theory as human science.* New York: Gardner Press, 1976.

Eiben, R., & Milliren, A. (Eds.). *Educational change: A humanistic approach.* San Diego, CA: University Associates, 1976.

Ellis, S.J., & Noyes, K.H. *By the people: A history of Americans as volunteers.* Philadelphia, PA: Energize, 1978.

Firestone, S. *The dialectic of sex: The case for feminist revolution.* New York: William Morrow, 1970.

Fletcher, J. *Situation ethics.* Philadelphia, PA: Westminster Press, 1966.

Galbraith, J.K. *The affluent society.* Boston, MA: Houghton Mifflin, 1976.

Galbraith, J.K. *Economic development.* Cambridge, MA: Harvard University Press, 1964.

Gowan, S. *Moving toward a new society.* Philadelphia, PA: New Society Press, 1976.

Gregory, D. *Nigger.* New York: E.P. Dutton, 1964.

Griffin, J. *Black like me.* New York: New American Library, 1961.

Hallman, H.W. *Neighborhood government in a metropolitan setting.* Beverly Hills, CA: Sage, 1974.

Hallman, H.W. *The organization and operation of neighborhood councils.* New York: Praeger, 1977.

Harrington, M. *The other America.* New York: Macmillan, 1962.

Haveman, R.H. *A decade of federal antipoverty programs.* New York: Academic Press, 1977.

Hutchinson, L., & Wasserman, M. *Teaching human dignity.* Minneapolis, MN: Education Exploration Center, 1978. (Can be obtained from Education Exploration Center, 3104 16th Avenue South, Minneapolis, MN 55408.)

Jacobs, J. *The death and life of great American cities.* New York: Random House, 1961.

King, M.L., Jr. *Stride toward freedom.* New York: Harper & Row, 1958.

King, M.L., Jr. *Where do we go from here: Chaos or community.* New York: Harper & Row, 1967.

Knowles, L., & Prewitt, K. *Institutional racism in America.* Englewood Cliffs, NJ: Prentice-Hall, 1969.

Kotler, M. *Neighborhood government: The local foundations of political life.* Indianapolis: Bobbs-Merrill, 1960.

Langton, S. (Ed.). *Citizen participation perspectives: Proceedings of the national conference on citizen participation.* Medford, MA: Lincoln Filene Center for Citizenship and Public Affairs, Tufts University, 1979.

Malcolm X. *Autobiography.* New York: Grove Press, 1964.

Meadows, D.H. et al. *The limits of growth: A report for the Club of Rome's project on the predicament of mankind* (2nd ed.). New York: Universe Press, 1974.

Morgan, R. *Sisterhood is powerful: An anthology of writings from the women's liberation movement.* New York: Vintage, 1970.

Morris, D., & Hess, K. *Neighborhood power: The new localism.* Boston, MA: Beacon Press, 1975.

Moynihan, D.P. *Maximum feasible misunderstanding.* New York: Free Press, 1969.

Murray, E., & Webb, L. (Eds.). *New directions in state and local public policy.* Washington, DC: Conference on Alternative State and Local Public Policies, 1977.

Nader, R., & Ross, D. *Action for a change.* New York: Grossman, 1972.

Owens, R.G. *Organizational behavior in schools.* Englewood Cliffs, NJ: Prentice-Hall, 1970.

People power: What communities are doing to counter inflation. Washington, DC: U.S. Office of Consumer Affairs, 1980. (Can be obtained from Consumer Information Division, 621 Reporters Building, Washington, DC 20201.)

Sarason, S.B. *The creation of settings and the future societies.* San Francisco: Jossey-Bass, 1972.

Schindler-Rainman, E., & Lippitt, R. *The volunteer community: Creative use of human resources* (2nd ed.). San Diego, CA: University Associates, 1975.

Schumacher, E.F. *Small is beautiful.* New York: Harper Torchbooks, 1973.

Shalala, D.E. *Neighborhood governance: Issues and proposals.* New York: National Project on Ethnic America, 1971.

Stereotypes, distortions, and omissions in U.S. history textbooks. New York: Council on Interracial Books for Children, 1970.

Taking charge. San Francisco: American Friends Service Committee, The Simple Living Collective, 1977.

The tarnished golden door: Civil rights issues in immigration. Washington, DC: U.S. Commission on Civil Rights, Government Printing Office, 1980.

Terry, R. *For whites only.* Detroit: Detroit Industrial Mission, 1970.

Theobald, R. *Beyond despair: Directions for America's third century.* Washington, DC: New Republic Book Company, 1976.

Theobald, R. *Futures conditional.* Indianapolis: Bobbs-Merrill, 1972.

Theobald, R. *Habit and habitat.* Englewood Cliffs, NJ: Prentice-Hall, 1972.

Theobald, R. *Rich and poor: A study of the economics of rising expectations.* New York: Potter, 1960.

Toffler, A. *Future shock.* New York: Random House, 1970.

Voices from Wounded Knee, 1973. Akwesasne, NY: Akwesasne Notes, 1973. (Can be obtained from Mohawk Nation, Rooseveltown, NY 13683.)

CONSCIOUSNESS

Bateson, G. *Steps to an ecology of mind*. New York: Ballantine, 1975.

Boyd, D. *Rolling thunder*. New York: Random House, 1974.

Boyd, D. *Swami*. New York: Random House, 1976.

Buber, M. *I and thou*. New York: Charles Scribner's, 1958.

Castaneda, C. *Journey to Ixtlan*. New York: Simon & Schuster, 1972.

Castaneda, C. *Tales of power*. New York: Simon & Schuster, 1974.

Glasser, W. *Positive addiction*. New York: Harper & Row, 1976.

Kubler-Ross, E. *Death: The final stage of growth*. Englewood Cliffs, NJ: Prentice-Hall, 1975.

Lame Deer, J., & Erdoes, R. *Lame Deer: Seeker of visions*. New York: Simon & Schuster, 1972.

Maltz, M. *Psycho-cybernetics*. Englewood Cliffs, NJ: Prentice-Hall, 1960.

Moss, T.S. *The probability of the impossible*. Los Angeles: J.P. Tarcher, 1974.

Pearce, J.C. *The crack in the cosmic egg*. New York: Julian Press, 1971.

Pearce, J.C. *Magical child: Rediscovery of nature's plan for our children*. New York: E.P. Dutton, 1975.

Pirsig, R. *Zen and the art of motorcycle maintenance*. New York: William Morrow, 1974.

Reich, C.A. *The greening of America*. New York: Random House, 1970.

Robbins, R. *Even cowgirls get the blues*. Boston, MA: Houghton Mifflin, 1976.

Teilhard de Chardin, P. *The phenomenon of man*. New York: Harper & Row, 1959.

Thompson, H.S. *Fear and loathing in Las Vegas*. New York: Random House, 1971.

INDEX

Please add the following name to your mailing list.

UA

_____

_____

_____

_____ Zip _____

Primary Organizational Affiliation: [ ] fill in with one number from below

1. Education
2. Business & Industry
3. Religious Organization
4. Government Agency
5. Counseling

6. Mental Health
7. Community, Voluntary, and/or Service Organization
8. Health Care
9. Library
0. Consulting

Please add the following name to your mailing list.

UA

_____

_____

_____

_____ Zip _____

Primary Organizational Affiliation: [ ] fill in with one number from below

1. Education
2. Business & Industry
3. Religious Organization
4. Government Agency
5. Counseling

6. Mental Health
7. Community, Voluntary, and/or Service Organization
8. Health Care
9. Library
0. Consulting